Battleground

CAMB
The Right H

With the continued expansion of the Battleground series a **Battleground Europe Club** has been formed to benefit the reader. The purpose ⟨
Club is to keep members informed of new titles and key developments by way of a quarterly newsletter, and to offer many other reader-be⟨
Membership is free and by registering an interest you can help us predict print runs and thus maintain prices at their present levels. Please ca⟨
office 01226 734555, or send your name and address along with a request for more information to:
Battleground Europe Club
Pen & Sword Books Ltd, 47 Church Street, Barnsley, South Yorkshire S70 2AS

Battleground Europe

CAMBRAI
The Right Hook

Jack Horsfall & Nigel Cave

Series editor
Nigel Cave

LEO COOPER

This guide is dedicated to all those who fought for allied arms in this small region of France: to the Contemptible Little Army in 1914; to the French army and the local civilians; to the Welsh battalions in the spring of 1917 who pushed the Germans back to the Flanders Sanatorium; and those who took part in the preparation for, and participated in, the two battles for the Hindenburg Line and the St Quentin canal.

First published in 1999 by
LEO COOPER
an imprint of
Pen Sword Books Limited
47 Church Street, Barnsley, South Yorkshire S70 2AS

ISBN 0 85052 632 9

A CIP catalogue of this book is available
from the British Library

Printed by Redwood Books Limited
Trowbridge, Wiltshire

For up-to-date information on other titles produced under the Leo Cooper imprint, please telephone or write to:
Pen & Sword Books Ltd, FREEPOST, 47 Church Street
Barnsley, South Yorkshire S70 2AS
Telephone 01226 734222

CONTENTS

Introduction by Series Editor

Cambrai, The Right Hook

Cambrai is amongst the best known battle names from the Great War; it is possibly one of the least visited battlefield sites. This is strange for a number of reasons. It is hard by the Somme battlefield - about a twenty to thirty minute drive from Bapaume will bring you into the midst of the late November 1917 battle zone. The countryside over which the battle was fought remains largely agricultural. The cemeteries and villages mark out the salient points of the fighting, and the new(ish) motorway does not really hinder an understanding of the battlefield. It is quite a straightforward battle to follow on the ground, and there are plenty of sharp engagements in the relatively open warfare that took place in this epic stroke and counterstroke to provide interesting and informative battlefield walks and drives. The area can be a little bleak, but the landscape is varying and there are numerous places of interest, such as Vaucelles Abbey, Cambrai itself and along the Canal du Nord. There are even quite a substantial number of physical remnants from the war. There are plenty of places to stay, even if the traveller lacks the intrepid spirit to tackle rush hour in Cambrai.

It would seem that the element that is missing is a good guide to the area. I can honestly say that this book deals admirably with the events on the right flank of the attack. I can say this without being a braggart as all the hard work for this book has been done by Jack Horsfall. The guide outlines the main details of the battles in November and December 1917 and the events as the war came to its last gasp in the early autumn of 1918, interspersed with accounts of individuals and of stories of tragedy and horror from 1914.

Cambrai is an important battle, still awaiting a full academic survey. The British failure in late November is important, though valuable lessons were learnt from the experience (whatever the limitations of the post-battle enquiry might have been). In some respects the failure of the German counter-stroke was of equal significance, and this aspect in particular could do with a systematic study. A decent biography in English is still awaited of Crown Prince Rupprecht of Bavaria, who for much of the war was the British army's principal enemy commander on the Western Front.

The British assault in this sector was effectively over within forty-eight hours of its start, rather as Haig had lain down if it failed to achieve the desired results. Although battles are grand designs involving thousands upon thousands of men, much could depend on fate in very small actions. In this case it could be a matter of a tank getting across a partly damaged bridge, or of a tank commander making the right decision about the employment of his four machines, or of a resolute officer launching almost a solo counter-attack against advancing Germans. What makes the study of battlefield actions on the ground so fascinating is a mixture of the massive, and the great issues at stake, and the activities of small groups of men or of individuals – almost a matter of bringing the ghastliness of the whole down to a scale with which we can empathise as human beings.

Although the number of battlefield visitors here is small, the local authorities have awoken to the fact that stirring events took place in this Cambresis region of France, and they have now put into position a tour route. The explanatory notices are useful, with accompanying map, contemporary photographs and a text in both French and English. The people 'of the right hook' have always, in my experience, been welcoming and helpful; I would ask that visitors respect their fields and their tracks and be considerate of the needs of the local population – people wandering over crops, leaving their vehicles parked so as to block tracks and crashing into woodland are as unwelcome here as they would be in Great Britain.

Nigel Cave
Ely Place, London

The ruins of La Vacquerie Church. For years the role of the small hamlets in the area during the war was neglected but now the Tourist Board has established a memorial route around them.

Acknowledgements

The story in the guide is the result of other men's labours, and therefore to whom grateful thanks are due – the regimental and divisional historians, the writers and compilers of War Diaries and the authors of personal reminiscences. Local historians in France have produced works on the ambush at Bonavis in 1914 and of events in 1944 in Flesquieres. To these must be added regimental secretaries and the helpful and patient assistance rendered by the various departments of the Imperial War Museum, most notably the Department of Photography.

The Commonwealth War Graves Commission both in the UK and Canada were most helpful, lending numerous registers and providing details of Victoria Cross winners; these registers also ensured that early casualties of 1914, buried in communal cemeteries, were not lost when the ground work was done for this book.

Particular thanks are due to M Arnaud Gabet of Les Rues des Vignes and M Jean Luc Gibot of Gouzeaucourt for their freely given knowledge of war time events at Crevecoeur and Ligny en Cambresis.

After the battle: two German soldiers examine a knocked out 'male' British tank. Although a vital part of the attack, the tank was slow, cumbersome and highly vulnerable to artillery fire.

Advice for Tourers

This very important battlefield is off the beaten track for the majority of visitors to the Western Front. This is something of a pity, for it is easily accessible and lies in some beautiful and undisturbed country.

The approach is best via the commonly used route to the Somme - except at Bapaume, instead of heading west to the Somme, head east towards Cambrai. It is, of course, quite possible to combine a visit to the two battlefields and base yourself on the Somme.

Somme Accommodation suggestions:
    Hotel de la Paix, 62450 Bapaume Tel +33 321 07 11 03
    Hotel le Prieure, 60360 Rancourt Tel +33 322 85 04 43
These hotels have the advantage of being midway between the two battlefields.

Bed and Breakfast Accommodation:
    Julie Renshaw, Les Galets, Route de Beaumont, 80560
    Auchonvillers. Tel/Fax +33 422 76 28 79
    Avril Williams, 10 Rue de Lattre, 80560 Auchonvillers.
    Tel +33 322 76 23 66

In fact there are numerous other B & Bs, Gites and campsites on the Somme – a full list may be obtained from the Comité Regional du Tourisme de Picardie, 3 Rue Vincent Auriol, 80000 Amiens Tel +33 322 91 10 15.

On the Cambrai battlefield there is, to my knowledge, at the moment no British run accommodation, but events might have overtaken me in this regard! There are numerous hotels in Cambrai, including an Ibis and a Campanile on the Bapaume road.

In Marcoing there is a Hotel/restaurant on the old station square, 26, Place de la Gare, 59159 Marcoing Tel +33 327 79 46 78; it has a number of small, quite adequate, rooms.

There are quite a number of Chambre d'Hotes/ B & B places on the battlefield area.
    La Ferme de Bonavis , Carrefour RN44 et D917, 59266
    Banteux. Tel +33 327 78 55 08.
    Ferme des Ecarts, Les Rues des Vignes, 59241 Masnieres.
    Tel +33 327 37 51 10.
    M et Mme Denimal, 386 Rue de Cambrai, 59266 Banteux.
    Tel +33 327 78 50 63
    M et Mme Pisselet, 482 Rue du Milieu, 59266 Banteux.

Tel +33 327 76 50 05
M et Mme Douy, 2 Rue de Cambrai, 59266 Banteux.
Tel +33 327 76 50 03

Attempts have been made to be as accurate as possible, and apologies are offered if any errors have crept in.

The standard travel advice as regards vehicle and personal insurance is offered – ensure that your insurance covers Europe (it usually does now), take suitable breakdown cover and take out personal insurance. Reciprocal medical cover is available by procuring an E1 11, but you should be warned that the French health insurance system is not as all-embracing as ours, and you might find yourself paying substantial charges, especially as often you are required to pay a bill first and then claim the money back later. Ensure that your tetanus booster is up to date.

The battlefield can be both a cold and a very hot place. Take a rucksack with you with suitable waterproof clothing and a hat is advised regardless of the weather. Sun cream and water are recommended, especially if you are off on a long walk. In your rucksack you would be advised to have binoculars, camera, note book and a compass, as well as relevant maps. The necessaries for a picnic lunch are plentiful and available from fairly frequent shops – but do not forget to carry a bottle opener and suitable drinking vessels – as well as a corkscrew – in the car.

The tours and walks do not take you, necessarily, over very difficult ground. However stout shoes, well broken-in, are strongly recommended. Keep a plastic bag in the car in which to put muddy footwear on your return to the vehicle.

Ensure you have basic spare parts for the vehicle, two warning triangles (the law on this varies from state to state) and a first aid kit.

The maps for the tour should be adequate. A good navigation map is the French Green Series No 4, Arras – Laon; the Blue Series maps are 2507 est and 2607 ouest. Trench maps may be obtained from the Western Front Association (if you are a member) – where, also, the more commonly required Blue Series maps may also be obtained. For details about membership write to: The Western Front Association, PO Box 1914, Reading, Berks RG4 7YP. The Commonwealth War Graves Commission produces a number of overprinted Michelin 1:200000 maps showing the locations of the vast majority of British burial grounds with an accompanying index. These cost £3 each (the one for this area is No 53) and are available from The Commonwealth War Graves Commission, 2 Marlow Road, Maidenhead, Berks SL6 7DX.

Tel 01628 634221. They can also help you with casualty queries, for which a small charge may be made; and it is also possible to access the database for details of casualties on the internet (www.cwg.org).

We would urge you to be aware of those whose economic livelihood depends on the land and to avoid leaving your car in a position where it might obstruct other vehicles, and especially agricultural vehicles. Respect the land, especially with crops on it, and private property. Be conscious of the dangers of the hunting season, when you are liable to be blasted at from every direction (nothing personal, of course). Woods must be approached with especial caution, and again it is best to seek permission before diving in, and do please keep to the paths.

Munitions remain potentially lethal; the best advice is to leave them alone. It is an offence in French law to have them on your person or in a vehicle, and the penalties can be harsh, including the confiscation of the vehicle carrying them. I am unsure about the law on metal detectors in this part of France, but at the very least permission of the landowner would be a minimum requirement.

In the recent past this battlefield has begun to be covered by the Battleground Europe series. A good general survey is Peter Oldham's *Hindenburg Line*, and already published are Bill Mitchinson's more detailed *Epehy*, *Riqueval*, and *Villers Plouich*. It is always useful to have Rose Coombs' *Before Endeavours Fade* with you.

The Germans retrieved British tanks, repaired them and used them themselves, but only on a limited scale. They did construct their own tanks in due course but generally they were ineffectual. The German High Command was never convinced of their value.

LIST OF MAPS

This explanatory plaque in front of the church at La Vacquerie is one of eleven erected in the villages and hamlets of the southern part of the Cambrai battlefield.

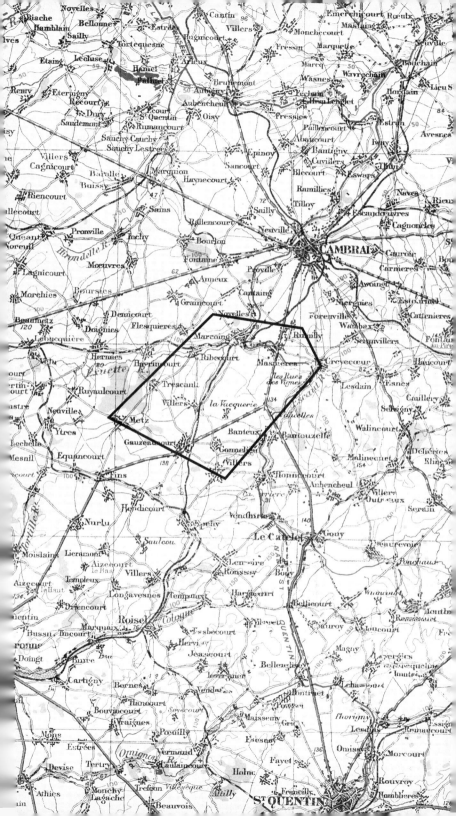

Chapter One

SETTING THE SCENE: THE STORY OF THE BATTLE

The ancient town of Bapaume, practically destroyed in the First World War and badly battered in the Second, sits on an historical crossroads. It is approximately halfway between Arras and Peronne on the north to south road; and halfway between Cambrai and Amiens on the east to west Roman road and is fifteen to twenty miles from each of them.

To the east of Bapaume the land is flat and dotted with numerous small villages, many still based on the agriculture that was their purpose before the war. Each usually has a disproportionately large church, orchards and a wood, and they lie a mile or so from their neighbour.

About ten miles from Bapaume is the settlement of Metz en Couture, and from here the landscape changes quite dramatically. Several hundred yards to its north is the southern edge of Havrincourt Wood. The great forest dominates as the road rises up a ridge to the village of Trescault. This is a suitable point from which to view the battlefield.

From here the land rolls in a series of valleys. To the north are the villages of Havrincourt and Flesquieres, with the spires of Cambrai in the far distance, some six miles to the north east of them. To the east is a long valley, at the base of which is a shallow drainage ditch, which gives the valley its name of Grand Ravin. The valley runs through Ribecourt, some two miles away, and on to Marcoing. To the south the valley gradually rises towards the village of Beaucamp, about a mile and a half away. Another notable feature of the area is two artificial waterways. The Canal du Nord enters a long tunnel at Ytres, three miles west of Metz; it emerges at Ruyaulcourt. Thence it goes round the western edge of Havrincourt Wood and proceeds through a ninety foot cutting to the west of Havrincourt itself, finally connecting to the Sensee River some miles to the north. The Canal was under construction in 1914, and was therefore dry, although still a most formidable obstacle. Five miles to the east, over the Couillet and Bonavis ridges, there is a deep valley through which winds the St Quentin Canal. This canal begins far to the south, beyond Compiegne and comes north up to and through the western edge of Cambrai,

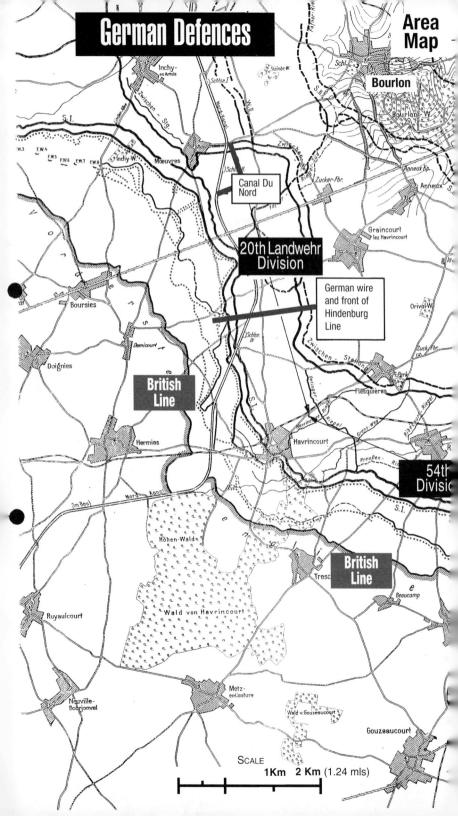

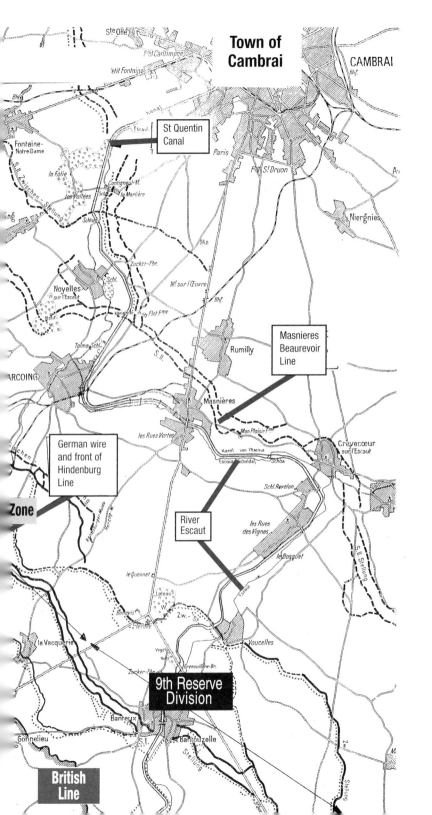

almost parallel to the Canal du Nord, before itself joining with the Sensee. In the area of interest in this book, the small River Escaut flows, rising at Gouy, some twenty miles south of Cambrai.

In the later months of 1916 and early in 1917 the Germans built a formidable defensive line stretching from the Arras area in a south easterly direction, incorporating Havrincourt and the ready-made obstacle of the Canal du Nord and proceeding before Trescault, on the eastern side. It then climbed the Couillet and Bonavis ridges and then followed the St Quentin Canal, going south for many miles. The strongest section of the system lay before you, crossing the valleys and ridges only a few hundred yards from Trescault. At this point it was five miles deep, with row upon row of heavy gauge barbed wire barricades and deep trenches, purposely dug very wide to inhibit the passage of tanks. The Germans called the system the Siegfried Stellung; the British named it the Hindenburg Line.

The construction and development of the Hindenburg Line, as well as a detailed examination of the remnants visible today, is covered by Peter Oldham's *Hindenburg Line* in this series; further details may be found in Bill Mitchinson's set of books, also in the series, on *Riqueval, Epehy* and *Villers Plouich*.

In brief, the Germans determined that holding the salient created by the ferocious battles of the Somme throughout the summer and autumn of 1916 required an inefficient and unsustainable use of manpower, and determined to withdraw to prepared positions to the east – positions which would be impregnable, at least to the attack methods used to date. They began a withdrawal from the old Somme positions in late February 1917, and in a most skilful withdrawal moved eastwards, inflicting numerous casualties on the pursuing armies. In addition they set about a destruction of villages, farmhouses, road crossings, wells, orchards – of anything that could be of any value – that was the most ruthless example of a scorched earth policy that had been seen. So severe was this that it almost led to the resignation of Crown Prince Rupprecht of Bavaria, one of the most successful of Germany's Army Commanders. By May the German troops were safely ensconced behind their vast defensive system.

The five mile, north south, stretch ahead of you has changed little since the Great War. The villages did not suffer the fate of total obliteration as did those between Bapaume and Metz, and they have all been restored from the significant damage that they did endure. Almost all traces of the Hindenburg Line have been erased, although enough remains to give some impression of the extent of this defensive system.

The formidable German command team of Ludendorff (left) and von Hindenburg.

Farms have been restored on their old foundations; many of them were converted into strongpoints, their cellars reinforced with metal and concrete. Most of the tracks and roads remain, most (but by no means all!) are passable in a car – indeed some of these by ways formed part of the line. It is important to remember that nearly all of the roads would have been significantly narrower than today (this applies especially to the main roads), and many would have been deeper, shielded by steep embankments on either side. They would either have been chalk and clay tracks or, at best, have a centre part made of pavé, laid in a most awkward concave fashion, making it both difficult and uncomfortable for marching bodies of troops. All over the area there is the hallmark of this part of the old Western Front; the numerous cemeteries, many small and isolated, of the Commonwealth War Graves Commission.

Cambrai is now a large industrial town of some forty thousand souls – about twice the number that lived there in 1914. It has a historic connection well before the Great War with the British, for it was here that the series of treaties known as the Treaty of Cateau Cambresis were signed in 1559 that ended a long war that had involved France, the Empire, Spain and England. It still has the air of an ancient town, despite the heavy damage it suffered in 1917 and 1918, particularly from the retreating Germans in 1918. Once encircled by walls, these have now generally gone, to make way for roads and railway, though a number of its splendid towers and gates survive. It is

German delayed action mine exploding in Cambrai after they had departed.
TAYLOR LIBRARY

This intricate stonework in Cambrai survived the German occupation and its capture 1918. TAYLOR LIBRARY

still an important rail centre, with good road connections and conveniently connected to the autoroute system, making it an ideal and interesting town from which to explore this part of north eastern France.

At the end of 1914 it was made into a great reinforcement base for German troops, sending men up to the Salient and to the battlefields of the Somme to the south. It had good communications back into Germany whilst, until the withdrawal from the 1916 Somme line, it was many miles behind front line activity and only had to endure the occasional pinprick of annoyance from the early gestation of air raids and aerial bombing. Although now much closer to the front, the Hindenburg Line was designed, amongst other things, to ensure its security and that of the countryside around it. For much of the war the villages around about had provided a rest area for troops from the front – so much so that it was known as the 'Flanders Sanatorium'.

Secure in its earthworks, concrete emplacements, well sited artillery pieces and machine-guns, it was considered that the line here could be held by a couple of second line divisions – sufficient to safeguard against British patrolling activities, a foe who would realise the severe limitations imposed upon their actions by the extraordinary mass of barbed wire facing them. In any case, it would take the British months to restore a logistical network to support the men in the trenches, let alone preparing for any sort of offensive. The British cemeteries at Neuville Bourjonval, Ruyaulcourt and other villages close to, or west of, the Hindenburg Line in the corridor heading back towards Bapaume, bear sad witness to the efficacy of the German artillery, relatively secure in its valley positions.

The British Commander in Chief, Field Marshal Sir Douglas Haig, had long known of Cambrai's importance, but its distance from the 1916 front had always been so great as to preclude planning operations against it. The German withdrawal in the spring of 1917 brought the town tantalisingly close to his Fourth Army. However he was committed to his cherished offensive in Flanders, Third Ypres, popularly known as Passchendaele, and any operations in this sector would be secondary to that.

During April, whilst the Battle of Arras was being fought, at a conference of the British and French Commanders in Chief, it was proposed by General Nivelle that the two armies should launch a simultaneous attack close to St Quentin, with the British taking the northern sector in the vicinity of Havrincourt. This proposal was acceptable to Haig, as it meant that the French did not intend to close

Field Marshal Sir Douglas Haig

General Nivelle

Lieutenant General Sir Julian Byng

down their offensives after the setbacks of the year.

Following from this French suggestion, Haig ordered his Fourth and Fifth Army staffs to make plans for an assault on the Hindenburg Line. In the first week of May the two Army commanders, Rawlinson (Fourth) and Gough (Fifth) began to examine the proposals. Later in the month he was able to inform the French Commander in Chief at a meeting in Amiens that plans for an assault on the Hindenburg Line were in motion. In June the Fourth Army was moved to Flanders, to take part in operations there; Third Army, whose reserve area was at Achiet le Petit, north west of Bapaume, took over the sector north and south of Havrincourt, with the Fifth Army on its right, above and below Peronne.

The Third Army had been heavily involved in the Battle of Arras; its new commander was Julian Byng, whose Canadian Corps (then serving under Horne's First Army) had had an outstanding success in capturing Vimy Ridge in the opening days of the Arras offensive. A major contributor to his Corps' success lay in the carefully planned artillery programme, a lesson which he would carry forward to Cambrai.

Another enthusiast for an offensive in the Army's new sector was the young (forty years old) and dynamic Brigadier-General HJ Elles, a Royal Engineer officer commanding the Tank Corps in France. Equally eager to see the tank fighting over this sort of 'ideal' ground for the new weapon was Elles' chief of staff, Lieutenant-Colonel JFC Fuller.

Meanwhile Brigadier-General HH Tudor, BGRA (Brigadier-General Royal Artillery, ie the artillery commander) of the 9th (Scottish) Division, part of IV Corps, also in the Cambrai sector, came up with a novel idea of his own. He suggested a diversion, on a relatively small scale, and therefore sustainable with the military resources available, from the Ypres offensive in the north, which would attract the Germans' attention to Cambrai.

To secure surprise he advocated that reliance be placed upon survey methods of gun-laying instead of allowing preliminary registration by the usual practice of trial and error with ground and air observation; and that the tanks should crush passages through wire for the infantry when the sudden assault was delivered. Thus no wire - cutting would be required and no guns need open fire before the actual zero hour.[1]

Nothing came of the various proposals at this stage other than a recommendation that the Tank Corps and the artillery should work together to smash a way through the vast barbed wire barricades; and that the area south of Havrincourt (including the wood) should be reconnoitred to assess the feasibility of assembling a large quantity of tanks and artillery there.

In September Byng, who was very enthusiastic about a surprise attack with tanks and artillery, was told to go into more detail with the scheme, but again was impressed with the need for absolute secrecy. On no account should any preparations he might consider necessary to make be seen by the enemy or be obvious to his own troops.

Winter was fast approaching, a season which would preclude Haig from launching an offensive anywhere on his front. With the failure of the attack of 12 October at Ypres, Byng's proposals for his assault were approved, and he was instructed to proceed in detail but still under conditions of great secrecy. The problems at Ypres were compounded by other pressures. On 24 October a combined Austro-German offensive at Caporetto, on the Italian front, achieved considerable and dramatic success in terms of ground gained and the scale of casualties inflicted upon the Italians. Haig was instructed to send, immediately, two divisions to Italy, with a further two divisions, batteries of heavy artillery and squadrons of the RFC to follow. In addition, General Plumer, who had been conducting operations in the southern part of the attack at Ypres, was instructed to go to Italy as commander of the British troops.

If that were not enough, the British had also promised to take over more of the front held by the French, themselves recovering from the morale lowering mutinies of earlier in the year.

Finally, by this stage in the war the relationship between the brasshats (the generals) and the frocks (the politicians), notably that between Haig and Robertson (Chief of the Imperial General Staff) on the one side and Lloyd George, the Prime Minister, on the other, had become poisonous.

Haig decided that the offensive at Cambrai was to go ahead, despite all the difficulties. The staff work for the attack was very fine; never before on the Western Front had so much heavy equipment, armoured fighting vehicles and artillery been gathered together with all their associated vehicles, ammunition, tools, vast dumps of oil, water, petrol and stores and been moved so far forward to the enemy without being detected.

In addition nineteen divisions of infantry, four of cavalry and three brigades of tanks not only had to be put in place but all of them moved in and out of the Army's rear area to be trained in the technique of working with tanks.

The operational planning would have to be completed in a matter of a few weeks; secrecy was maintained and a disinformation series of measures were put in place. For example, Italian speaking officers were called for to go to the Tank Corps training ground. Meanwhile railway lines had to be laid to move men, equipment, tanks and road making materials; accommodation had to be built. Engineers and pioneers prepared camps and camouflaged them with tens of thousands of square yards of netting; water points were built in an area where there were no rivers and all the wells had been poisoned; tracks and roads were built and full gauge and light railways established. Signallers laid almost two hundred miles of communication cables to division and brigade headquarters. Horses and mules also needed vast quantities of forage and water. The November weather helped in this process, as the dull, misty and rainy conditions impeded German aerial and balloon observation.

To ensure that the artillery could carry out the type of fire that Tudor had recommended a detailed and extremely accurate survey had to be made; Byng was adamant that there would be no registration. The task of making this survey was left to Major BFE Keeling, whose achievement was quite outstanding. The method was not unheard of on the Western Front (indeed a primitive attempt had been made at Loos, two years earlier); the traditional approach would have been for a lengthy pre-attack barrage, usually lasting days. Whilst this served to destroy some elements of the defence – fortifications, gun positions and machine gun posts, and undermined the morale of the defending infantry – it made the intention of the attackers all too clear, allowing for suitable counter measures. In the case of the nature of the operations planned for Cambrai, in any case, it was essential that the ground be left as uncratered as possible – tanks found the going difficult enough without the added hazard of randomly scattered and deep shell holes.

Tank disabled in a shell hole. For the Cambrai attack there was to be no preliminary barrage, so as to avoid cratering the ground, for easier passage of the tanks.

Byng was to have the use of some one thousand guns – just over half of which would be 18 pdr. field guns and a limited number of huge calibre howitzers. These guns in particular had to be placed with extreme accuracy, with the barrel wear of individual guns being taken into account. Artillery boards had to be prepared for all the guns, showing the calculations for the targets. Because the barrage would consist of a great variety of phases and different types of shell – smoke, wire cutting, shrapnel, high explosive and different stages in the barrage – the detail required in Major Keeling's map making and surveying task was staggering. The squeeze for time is best illustrated by a comment in the Official History.

The last job was tackled at two o'clock on the morning of the battle when a 9.2-inch railway gun was placed in position on its specially constructed siding between Metz and Gouzeaucourt Wood. Its task was to enfilade a road, and accuracy of line was imperative. Working with torches and lamps from neighbouring trigonometrical points, the survey officer completed his task with little time to spare.

How true – there were well under four hours to spare, to be precise. On top of the surveying effort was the need to bring up close to a million rounds of ammunition. Today it is difficult to visualise how difficult it was to move such huge numbers and such a weight of ordnance – most of it done by natural muscle power, mule or human. Then there was the problem of keeping the ammunition clean. To talk in brief terms of an artillery barrage is to risk missing the ingenuity and sheer muscle power that lay behind it.

The tank was not either universally accepted or liked by the infantry. Their experience with them until now had been mixed – useful in part, but not to be relied upon. They were prone to breakdown, had been used in insufficient numbers, scattered amongst attacking formations and had been expected to perform over muddy – indeed boggy – ground, heavily cratered and trenched.

The Mark IV was the latest tank model. It was cumbersome and slow, with a speed of less than one mile an hour over rough going. Inside, the crew of eight had to put up with ghastly conditions – indescribable noise and overpowering fumes. However, the men of the Tank Corps had all the enthusiasm and determination of Old Testament prophets, convinced of the tanks' war-winning potential, defects and all. Cambrai would prove its worth because the ground, numbers of vehicles and tasks set were all within the new weapon's capabilities. It should smash down the deepest concentration of barbed wire ever created, destroy previously invincible machine-gun nests, overrun artillery positions and give the infantry a chance to achieve their objectives with greatly reduced casualties, as well as allowing the truly mobile arm, the cavalry, to have – at long last – a situation to exploit.

Elles amassed the largest concentration of tanks ever seen on a battlefield, denuding the rest of the front of every tank which he could make serviceable. He was determined that the tank should be seen for what he fervently believed it was –-the decisive weapon of the war. He managed to pull together 476 tanks. They would fight in nine battalions, each of these consisting of 36 tanks with six in reserve. These 378 fighting tanks would be supplemented by 54 supply tanks (petrol, oil, water and ammunition); 32 tasked with dragging barbed wire obstacles away, making paths for the cavalry; nine for communications, fitted with wireless; two with bridging equipment and one to bring telephone cable forward as the advance progressed.

The very wide trenches at the front of the Hindenburg Line required some form of bridging if the tanks were not to be stuck in them; the solution was the making of giant brushwood rolls (a fascine), carried

Preparations for Cambrai: tanks with facines to be used for trench bridging during the attack are brought up by rail.

on the front of a tank and dropped into the trench before the tank crossed. 400 tons of brushwood were gathered and suitable chain was procured by searching all over Britain. The 51st Chinese Labour Company set about making these up, along with the construction of 110 sledges to haul the various supplies that were required by the tanks.

Movement of the tank force and its equipment had to be by night; by 18 November 36 train loads of tanks and equipment had been deposited at, amongst others, Fins, Rocquigny and Ytres. On the evening of 19 November Brigadier-General Elles issued his famous Special Order No. 6.

Tomorrow the Tank Corps will have the chance for which it has been waiting for many months, to operate on good going in the van of the battle. All that hard work and the ingenuity can achieve has been done in the way of preparation. It remains for unit commanders and for tank crews to complete the work by judgement and pluck in the battle itself. In the light of past experience I leave the good name of the Corps with great confidence in these hands. I propose leading the attack of the centre division.

The Tank Corps was filled with pride. The fleet was going into battle led in person by its commander in his tank, a female, Hilda. He

was doing that extremely rare thing, a commander leading his men from the front (the wisdom of which could, of course, be called into question!). Elles had resolved to set the style for commanders in this new form of warfare. He went into battle with the brown, red and green Tank Corps flag (which he had designed in Cassel in August) flying from Hilda. He knew it would attract attention to his tank and be an inspiration to his men. It might be a new method of warfare, but Elles was reverting to the leadership methods used in battle in the seventeenth century and before.

About three hundred aircraft, a mixture of fighters and bombers, were available for the attack. These had a large range of tasks to carry out: attacking enemy aircraft, railway junctions, roads and concentrations of enemy troops; reporting (along with observation balloons) successes of the artillery and new targets; and, highly important, the movement of German

Brigadier General H J Elles was to set the style for his commanders by riding into battle with his men.

The arrival of the General's tank 'Hilda' at Méaulte two days before the commencement of the battle.

Special Order No 6.

1. Tomorrow the Tank Corps will have the chance for which it has been waiting for many months, — to operate on good going in the van of the battle.

2. All that hard work & ingenuity can achieve has been done in the way of preparation

3. It remains for unit commanders and for tank crews to complete the work by judgment & pluck in the battle itself.

4. In the light of past experience I leave the good name of the Corps with great confidence in their hands

5. I propose leading the attack of the centre division

Hugh Elles.
B.G.

19th Nov. 1917.   Commanding Tank Corps.

Distribution to. Tank Commanders.

Special Order Number 6 issued by General Elles on 19 November 1917.

Panoramic view of the terrain over which the attack on the German positions would be made.

reinforcements into the battle area.

Third Army was going to use two Corps for the attack, III and IV, with the main assault to be made by III Corps. On its right would be VII Corps, whose task it was to hold the flank with its 55th Division. IV Corps would have three of its divisions, the Guards, 2nd and 40th, in reserve before Bapaume. In total there would be nineteen divisions available, all of them battle hardened and most of them involved in the recent fighting around Ypres. III Corps was to use four divisions and its brigades and 52 battalions would each spend some two days in training, particularly in operating with tanks. As usual, the infantry were taken to scale models of the battleground, which in this case were laid out on the ground to the west of Bapaume. Trenches and wire barricades were built so that the Tank Corps could show the infantry how they would be surmounted. Mutual co-operation was essential, and the men had to trust the tanks enough to be confident of keeping close to them. Not all divisional commanders were convinced of the tactical methods being recommended; in this respect Harper (51st Division) has been most criticised, with Braithwaite (62nd) being a sceptic as well. Others carried out the training, but the time was insufficient to dispel entirely the poor reputation tanks had amongst the infantry,

The Cavalry Corps, under the command of Lieutenant-General Kavanagh, was situated south of Gouzeaucourt; although the idea of

using such an arm is alien to the modern mind, its speed and flexibility after a breakthrough had been achieved was essential – and, indeed, unique during the Great War – despite its obvious shortcomings and limitations in the face of the weaponry available to the defenders. Its task was to isolate Cambrai from the east, crossing the St Quentin canal and pushing northwards. The value of tanks in the breakthrough was fully appreciated, and the cavalry felt that they had a chance to

Moving into position. After a year of operating the tanks they do not seem to merit a second look from these troops. TAYLOR LIBRARY

British 18 pounders in action. Innovations in the British handling of artillery were a vital part of the battle plan.

British infantry moving along a communication trench to the front line.

show their worth for the first time since the frantic war of movement at the beginning of the war.

The plan, given the operational code, GY, was finalised on 13 November, after various amendments; it also operated under the strict proviso from Haig that he would stop it after forty eight hours, or if need be earlier, if it was not going as he thought it should.

Stage 1 involved the breaking of the Hindenburg Line and the securing of the canal crossings at Masnieres and Marcoing; then proceeding to the Masnieres-Beaurevoir line, the German Stellung II or second line.

Stage 2 required the cavalry

to advance through the gap, to isolate Cambrai, with the force seizing the crossings of the Sensee River and capturing Bourlon Wood, on its prominent height.

Stage 3 involved the clearing of Cambrai and the Quadrilateral and the elimination of German troops which had been cut off. This Quadrilateral was formed by the dry Canal du Nord in the west; the ridge and line in the south from Villers Plouich to the St Quentin Canal at Crevecoeur; a line northwards from Crevecoeur to the east of Cambrai; with the square completed by a line from there westwards to the Canal du Nord.

The front was 11,000 yards long; the day fixed for the battle, 20 November, was revealed in a Third Army order of 18 November, with zero (0620) fixed by another order on 19 November. The misty, dull weather of November played its part in the concentration of troops and machines to the front. Six divisions moved into the front line positions, but despite the racket created by such a movement, the Germans remained ignorant of what was going on.

To the north the 51st and 62nd Divisions of IV Corps were to capture Bourlon and Flesquieres, aided by 147 of the tanks. The key part of the attack lay with III Corps' four divisons, tasked with getting the cavalry across the St Quentin Canal rapidly – failure to achieve this would lead to the whole plan unravelling.

On the move to attack positions on the Hindenburg Line the photograph was taken some distance behind the front.

The 6th Division was waiting behind the Trescault Ridge, just to the west of Beaucamp; its advance would take it through Ribecourt in the valley bottom and then north eastwards towards Noyelles, on the left bank of the St Quentin canal. To its right was the 20th (Light) Division, coming out of the valley of Villers Plouich to climb the high Welch Ridge at the heavily defended hamlet of La Vacquerie; from here it would head down to the bridges crossing the St Quentin Canal at Crevecoeur, crossing a six mile stretch of enemy held country in the process. The right flank division of the Corps was the 12th (Eastern); it also was heading for the bridges, aiming for the village of Les Rues des Vignes, having first crossed the Bonavis ridge. Behind the 20th and the 12th divisions was the 29th, which would start a few hours after the others and which would also be engaged in the vital task of capturing bridges, in this case at Marcoing and Masnieres. These divisions would have 294 tanks attached to them.

Facing the British divisions on the eve of the attack between the Bapaume-Cambrai road and Havrincourt was the 20th Landwehr Division, which had only come into the sector a few days previously. Between Havrincourt and La Vacquerie was the 54th Division, which had arrived in August to recuperate in a 'quiet' zone after a difficult time in Ypres. These divisions had approximately six miles of front to hold; though they felt confident in the strength of the Siegfried Stellung to withstand any attack. To the south east of La Vacquerie was the 9th Reserve Division, which held a line six miles long down to Vendhuille; its right battalion would oppose the very edge of III Corps right flank division, the 12th. On the 19th the 107th Division, from the Russian Front, began to arrive in Cambrai.

The secrecy of British operations was not complete. Captured British prisoners on 18 November led the Germans to believe that an attack on Havrincourt was planned; a belief reinforced by the interception of the fragment of a telephone conversation. The Cambrai sector was reinforced by a regiment (effectively a brigade) and some artillery.

Once battle commenced, the Germans poured in reinforcements - immediately the 119th, 30th and 214th divisions were dispatched; a day later the 21st and 221st came into the battle. Others were subsequently brought into the action – the 34th, 220th, 28th, 49th (Reserve), 208th, 185th, 79th Reserve, 24th, 16th and the 10th divisions. By the end of the seventh day they had complete (or elements of) nineteen divisions at the battle zone, most of them fresh and the whole supported by a massive influx of artillery.

The remarkable success of the tank and the artillery plan enabled the infantry to advance in places up to eight thousand yards – the Siegfried defences had been broken.

By now Byng's men were tired, had suffered severe losses and were on the defensive. By this stage in the battle the pendulum had swung in favour of the Germans; and in hindsight it is easy to criticise the grand plan. Certainly the remarkable ability of the Germans to recover from a situation and to mobilise sufficient forces to launch counter-attacks was underestimated, despite plenty of British experience of this capacity. Perhaps Haig should have been content with his initial concept of a large scale raid to demonstrate the vulnerability of the Hindenburg Line not only to tanks but to well directed artillery.

On the other hand, the remarkable success of the tank, which enabled the infantry to advance ten thousand yards on a front of eleven thousand yards in only ten hours, and with casualties of only about four thousand men, was simply too awe-inspiring to be stopped. It was enough to cause the war time silence of church bells in Britain to be broken by peals of exuberant joy; it was enough for some over-enthusiastic souls to read, perhaps, too much into the capability of the tank. Numbers and operational capacity were both extremely limited, and the outstanding success of the artillery, ultimately the war winner, was in danger of being over shadowed.

Fatigue eventually brought the British attack to a halt, coupled with the durability and capability of the Germans. At the end of the nineteen days' long battle, however, the British infantry, despite their long time in the field, fought the Germans to a bloody standstill – for they made their own, unforced errors – and the British still held a large section of that 'invincible' defensive line. On 27 November Haig ordered the

Fatigue, coupled with the durability and capability of the Germans, eventually brought the British attack to a halt.

cessation of the offensive and the consolidation of the salient – some nine miles wide by four miles deep – forced into the enemy lines. In the German attacks that followed a skilful, hard fought, withdrawal left some fifty percent of that salient still in British hands when the battle finally drew to an unsatisfactory close on 7 December.

Lessons, of course, emerged from this battle, the first the British had fought on such a scale involving a long range, open battle of deep penetration into the enemy lines. Infantry should be lightly equipped to reduce fatigue; divisions should not necessarily keep in line, as the impetus was lost to the north of the attack when the 62nd hung back, waiting for the 51st Division to come up with them; whilst Headquarters at all levels needed to be much nearer to the front line in such fast moving warfare. Cambrai resulted in some 48,000 British and 53,000 German casualties. The battle was obviously disappointing in its outcome, but both the bold offensive and the well executed withdrawal were clear signs of the British army's ability to look at new strategic and tactical approaches to fighting. For the Germans it was another sign (Third Ypres was the first) that fixed lines of defence were vulnerable, no matter how well designed; an offensive was the only way in which they could hope to win the war.

The tank had emerged as a decisive weapon in warfare.

1. Wilfred Miles, *Official History: Military Operations France and Belgium 1917. The Battle of Cambrai* pp 6-7 *(OH)*

Chapter Two

THE FIRST DAY: THE BATTLES ON THE RIGHT FLANK, 20 NOVEMBER 1917

Much of the history of the battles around Cambrai in November and December 1917 dwells on the drive for Bourlon Wood and the area around the Bapaume-Cambrai road. This area falls outside this guide, which concentrates on the battle for the bridges between Marcoing and Les Rues des Vignes. This part of the action was carried out by three of the divisions – the 12th (Eastern), the 20th (Light) and the 29th (all part of III Corps) – and four battalions of the Tank Corps, along with elements of the Cavalry Corps. The task was to make it possible to pass through the infantry (who would have broken through the German lines) who, in turn, would encircle the town from the east in a knock-out punch – a right hook – and meet up with the divisions coming from the west.

If casualties are any indication of determined men fighting to achieve their objectives and showing dogged resistance in the face of

The tank had great potential but the conditions under which the crew worked were cramped, hot and noisy. Under fire metal splinters tended to fly around inside and even in ideal conditions it could only make four miles an hour.

crushing counter-attacks, then these three divisions had the lion's share. They suffered twenty five percent of the casualties in the long battle at Cambrai. To paraphrase a battle of 1944, the stone bridge at Crevecoeur, vital to the operation's success, was 'a bridge too far'.

At 8.40 am on the first day, 20 November, only two hours after the start of the attack, the 20th and 29th Divisions were specifically told that the Crevecoeur bridge must be taken as early as possible that day to enable the cavalry, waiting near La Vacquerie, to cross. Situated immediately in front of the village and crossing the River Escaut, the bridge is sheltered from an attack by a marsh between it and the canal. This narrow bridge defied General Byng in November 1917 and was to frustrate Major General Russell, commanding the New Zealand Division, in October 1918, forcing him to by-pass it.

The 12th Eastern Division:
Major General AB Scott
Order of Battle

35 Brigade:	36 Brigade:	37 Brigade:
(*Brigade-General B Vincent*)	(*Brigadier-General CS Owen*)	(*Brigadier-General AB Incledon-Webber*)
7/Norfolks	8/R Fusiliers	6/Queen's
7/Suffolks	9/R Fusiliers	6/West Kent
9/Essex	7/Sussex	7/East Surrey
5/Berks	11/Middlesex	6/East Kent
	Pioneers: 5/Northants	

---

20 November promised to be a typical autumnal day, a damp mist shrouding the landscape. The battlefield in front of the waiting men of the Division was almost empty of trees, with open fields gently rising up to a ridge some five thousand yards away. The Division was on the extreme right of III Corps' assault with its three brigades in and about the village of Gonnelieu, to the right of the old Roman road from Gouzeaucourt. Their objective that morning was the ridge; the ground they had to cross lay in a band running some five hundred yards to the left of the road and fifteen hundred yards to its right. Two miles to the east of their position lay the village of Banteux. In front of them, not more than five hundred yards, was the formidable Hindenburg Line. In addition to its rows of trenches and barbed wire – a defensive depth of

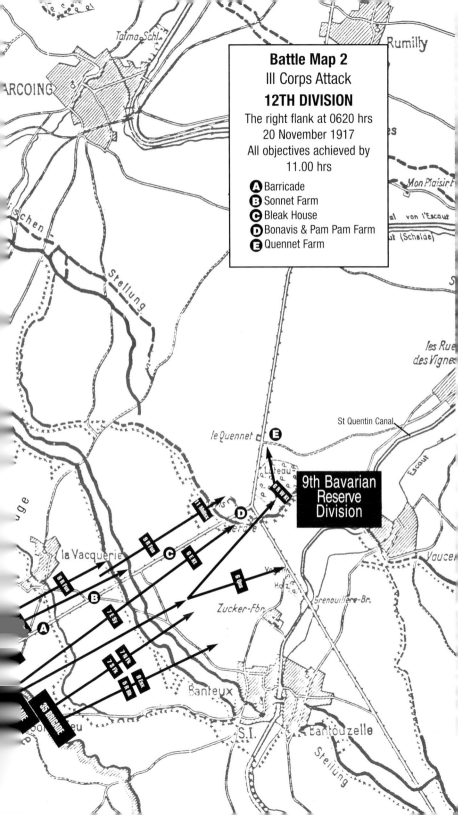

Battle Map 2
III Corps Attack
12TH DIVISION
The right flank at 0620 hrs
20 November 1917
All objectives achieved by
11.00 hrs

A Barricade
B Sonnet Farm
C Bleak House
D Bonavis & Pam Pam Farm
E Quennet Farm

9th Bavarian
Reserve
Division

35 BRIGADE

Sonnet Farm

Panoramic views of the battlefield which would have been available to British commanders well down the chain of command.

some five thousand yards – the Germans looked down on the British positions. The task was to break through the defences until they could see over the flat land on top of the ridge towards Cambrai, several miles to the north. They were then to form a defensive line on the right, in front of Banteux, looking down into the valley of the St Quentin Canal.

Included in the German defences were strong points, redoubts, which it was anticipated would cause difficulties. On the left flank of the divisional attack was the heavily fortified, tiny, hilltop village of La

Gauzeaucourt

Gonnil

The village of La Vacquerie played a prominent role in the battles of 1917 and 1918.

Vacquerie. Surrounded by trenches and deep dugouts, it formed a salient jutting out five hundred yards from the forward edge of the Hindenburg Line. In front of Banteux was a quarry, the home of many machine-guns, whilst straight ahead, and close to the main road, were a series of farm buildings, each heavily fortified. It would have been almost impossible to conceive of attacking such a front without the aid of a weapon such as the tank. The Germans expected an attack of some sort here, but in the late hours of Monday night were uncertain as to when. They had no idea what was to happen.

It had been decided that the tanks would attack on a broad front, contrary to Brigadier-General Elles's wishes; he wanted them to assault in 'spearheads' but the infantry generals wanted their protection – and assaulting power – along the whole width of the advance.

Shortly after 6am the tanks began their movement to the front line, the noise they made deliberately obscured by low flying aircraft. At 6.20am, as the tanks and infantry crossed into No Man's Land, the thousand pieces of artillery on the whole battle line opened fire on targets on which they had been scientifically registered over the battle zone between the two canals.

12th Division went forward. On its right, the extreme flank of Third Army's attack, was 35 Brigade, with 9/Essex and 5/Berks going for the ground north of Banteux. On their left came 7/Suffolks and 7/Norfolks, who broke through the Hindenburg Line south of Sonnet Farm. The tanks went before them, crushing the fearsome looking barbed wire flat. German defenders, stunned by the bombardment and

The early stages of the battle resulted in a considerable flood of German prisoners. The prisoners above were instructed to raise their hands for the benefit of the camera.

terrified by the 'iron monsters' rolling towards them, generally fled in panic, though some attempted, vainly, to stem the flow of the attack.

On the left 11/Middlesex led 36 Brigade attack up the main road and the land between it and La Vacquerie; following on were the 8 and 9/R Fusiliers and 7/Sussex, the Fusiliers taking the left flank of the Division. Storming through, behind the tanks, 8/Fusiliers took the outlying defences at La Vacquerie after the fortified farmhouse, the Barricade, had fallen; whilst the Royal Sussex, with tanks attached, attacked Bleak House on the main road. This particular fortress had escaped the bombardment and its defenders fought to the last. By 8am the Division had secured its first objective.

Shortly before 9am 37 Brigade took up the attack on the right with 7/East Surrey's leading the way with the supporting tanks essential to any progress forging ahead. Another of the fortresses, Le Pave, on the main road, at the front of the German's second line, was taken. Pam Pam Farm, deep in the Hindenburg second line, a few hundred yards to the north west of the Bonavis cross roads, was finally captured by 6/East Kents with the help of ten tanks, whose shell fire subdued it.

Meanwhile at the crossroads 11/Middlesex and half of 8/R Fusiliers took the large ruined farm of Bonavis, capturing a hundred and fifty prisoners, including a colonel and his staff, such was the speed of the advance. On the Division's right flank 6/Queen's and 6/RWK of 37 Brigade had been involved in heavy fighting whilst trying to establish the essential defensive line to the north and south of the crossroads.

Above the crossroads, and to the right of the road to Cambrai, was Lateau Wood, protected by another fortified farmhouse missed in the bombardment, Le Quennet Farm, five hundred yards further along the road on the left hand side. The wood had been hit by 12 inch shells as part of the artillery attack on Bonavis Farm. Both battalions were involved in fighting for the wood; 6/RWK on leaving it were fired upon from Le Quennet Farm. In this assault Major WJ Alderman was killed in the attack and capture of a 5.9 battery. His battalion went for the farm, becoming involved in very heavy fighting with its resolute defenders who eventually succeeded in overpowering the West Kents, taking many prisoners.

The Division's objectives had all been achieved in an advance of ,000 yards, during which twenty-five tanks had either been knocked out or were ditched. Nearly all the German 19th Reserve Regiment had been killed or captured, whilst Le Quennet Farm was evacuated by them a few hours later and was occupied by 37 Brigade.

The Division's initial task was completed before midday. Shortly afterwards two battalions of 37 Brigade, 6/Queen's and 6/RWK, at the Brigade's front and assisted by tanks of C Battalion, turned to the south east to set up forward posts overlooking the valley of the St Quentin canal. In the course of this action three of the tanks were knocked out by German artillery, firing at close range. Whatever hurried retreat the Germans might have made on the battlefront on that first day, their field artillery stood up well to the fearsome tank in their first anti-tank role and scored a number of close encounter successes. At the end of the Division's action on the 20th the Tank Corps managed to get together fifty five of the tanks they had committed to the sector. These now trundled forward to help the 29th Division as it came forward to battle for its objectives, the bridges on the St Quentin canal.

The 12th Division now started to deploy two of its brigades to face the south east, the southern flank of III Corps battle ground, preparing for the inevitable German counter attack. By the afternoon 37 Brigade was brought out of the line into reserve between La Vacquerie and Villers Plouich. 36 Brigade crossed the main road, taking up the Division's left flank, from Lateau Wood, east of Bonavis Farm and across the track down to Banteux. 35 Brigade withdrew west of the track and dug into the old German front line across the gently sloping land between Banteux and Villers Guislain.

A patrol of 7/Sussex went down into Banteux, crossed the bridge at the St Quentin canal lock and proceeded through the village of Bantouzelle without seeing any sign of the enemy.

The 12th (Eastern) Division's exciting day was over, but with many casualties, particularly to the West Kents.

A graphic illustration of the fact that tanks were vulnerable to well discipline artillery.

The 20th (Light) Division:
Major-General W Douglas Smith
Order of Battle

59 Brigade:	60 Brigade:	61 Brigade:
(*Brigade-General* *HHG Hyslop*)	(*Brigadier-General* *FJ Duncan*)	(*Brigadier-General* *WE Banbury*)
10/KRRC	6/Ox and Bucks	
11/KRRC	12/KRRC	7/SLI
10/RB	6/KSLI	7/DCLI
11/RB	12/RB	12/King's
		7/KOYLI

Pioneers: 11/DLI

With I and part of A battalions, Tank Corps, commanded by Colonel A Courage. 70 tanks, with fourteen for supplies.

The 20th (Light) Division was on the left flank of the 12th; 61 Brigade was on the right, adjacent to 36 Brigade. Alongside, on the left of the Division's 1700 yard front, was 60 Brigade; 59 Brigade was in reserve and not committed into the battle until 9.30 am.

The two front brigades, along with all the tanks allotted to the Division, went forward into the attack into the mist, following the artillery barrage. The task was to break through on the left, clearing the way for the 29th Division. On the right the objective was the heavily fortified salient of La Vacquerie, a small village on a hilltop, connected into the main Hindenburg Line by deep trenches with redoubts on each side; the whole surrounded by many strong barriers of barbed wire. During the preceding days the members of the Brigade had viewed the hamlet with some trepidation.

Their attack would be uphill over open ground, crossing the south end over the feature which had been named Welsh Ridge after the battles fought in April 1917 as the Royal Welsh Fusiliers and the South Wales Borderers pursued the Germans into the Siegfried Stellung.

7/DCLI's (Duke of Cornwall's Light Infantry) task was the capture of a redoubt, the Corner Work, which seemed most formidable. Appearances in this case were deceptive, for it fell very quickly, the stunning bombardment and the tanks being enough to force out the defenders into the main Hindenburg defences. Meanwhile 7/SLI (Somerset Light Infantry) made for the ruined church at the centre of the hamlet, which also fell with little loss. Then 7/SLI, two companies of 7/DCLI and half of 12/King's attacked the front of the main line, about five hundred yards east of the hamlet; there was resistance for a while, but, as the tanks crushed the wire, resistance petered out. By 10 am the Brigade had secured its first objective.

The Germans were now in the depth of the front section of the Hindenburg Line and would not give it up easily. The barrage had now passed over them, and the surprise element of the tank assault had run its course. The defenders had been bolstered by retreating troops from the outpost line and a number of reinforcements rushed up the line; whilst the artillery set about the slow moving tanks by firing at close range over open sights. The shooting knocked out eleven of the tanks within an hour, but 7/KOYLI (King's Own Yorkshire Light Infantry) and 12/King's had been used to being left to their own devices, and by 11.30 am were through the German lines.

On the left of 60 Brigade 6/Ox and Bucks and 12/KRRC (King's Royal Rifle Corps) also crossed Welsh Ridge; assisted by 18 tanks they attacked Corner Trench, taking their first objective, in the face of heavy resistance which cost A Company of 12/KRRC all its eight officers. It was here that 12/KRRC won its first VC of the war at Cambrai. Private Albert Shepherd, seeing that all his officers and NCOs had been hit and put out of action, took command of the men who were left, ordered his men to take cover and single-handedly rushed a machine-gun post. He then went to the rear to bring up a tank and with it led his men forward to take the trench whose occupants had caused so much destruction to his battalion. Shepherd went on to live many years, dying at Royston, near Barnsley, in 1966, at the age of 69.

Captain R W L Wain VC

With this obstacle removed, 6/KSLI (King's Shropshire Light Infantry) together with 12/RB (Rifle Brigade), and six tanks attacked the German second line almost a thousand yards ahead to the left, and north west of, Pam Pam and Bonavis farms. Once again their attack was met by determined German resistance against the tanks, their artillery well covered by nests of machine guns in the Hindenburg Support Line.

Captain Richard William Leslie Wain of I

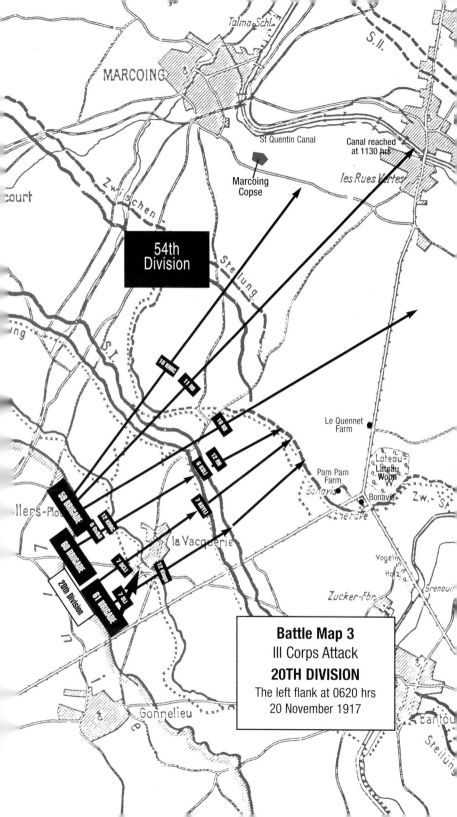

MARCOING

Talma Schl.

S. II.

St Quentin Canal

Canal reached
at 1130 hrs

les Rues Vertes

Marcoing
Copse

Zwischen-

court

Stellung

54th
Division

S. I.

10 KRRC

11 RB

Le Quennet
Farm

Lateau
Lateau
Wood

Zw.-St

10 DLI

12 RB

6 KSLI

Pam Pam
Farm

Bonavis

Bonavis

58 BRIGADE

12 KRRC

6 OxBR

7 DCLI

7 SLI

2 OYLI

Trescault

Vogel

Holz.

60 BRIGADE

20th Division

12 Kings

la Vacquerie

Zucker-Fbr.

61 BRIGADE

llers-Plo

L i n i e

Gonnelieu

Battle Map 3
III Corps Attack
20TH DIVISION
The left flank at 0620 hrs
20 November 1917

Steilung

Battalion, Tank Corps, his tank damaged by a direct hit, his crew killed or wounded and, despite being severely wounded himself, dismounted and took a Lewis gun, charged an enemy machine gun nest of five Maxim guns. He captured it and caused the remaining Germans to flee to the rear. Despite his serious injuries he picked up a rifle and shot at the fleeing enemy until he was again hit. Notwithstanding his desperate state, he stayed in action until he collapsed and died, but not before his tremendous bravery and resolute action allowed the infantry to take their objective. His body was not recovered, and he is commemorated on the Cambrai Memorial at Louverval.

Shortly afterwards, at 11 am, 60 Brigade secured its final objective.

59 Brigade started to move out of the valley and up the slope to the north of La Vacquerie shortly after 9 am. Its task was to extend the Division's front on the Bonavis Ridge and make for the Brown Line, three thousand yards ahead. When that was achieved it was to advance along the valley towards Masnieres, there to help the tanks already on their way to the St Quentin canal, which runs through the village. The three battalions in the lead (left to right: 10/KRRC, 11/RB and 10/RB) soon got into trouble at the German second line, which had not yet been attacked. However, within the hour they had gone through the Brown Line and were looking down the long slope to Masnieres. The small hamlet of Les Rues Vertes, part of the village in reality, but separated by the canal, lay directly in front of the lead battalion, 11/RB.

The place was not only occupied by the Germans, hiding in the buildings and using them as cover for their riflemen, but was also full of French civilians. With the help of one of the tanks the 11th entered the hamlet and forced the defenders to flee across the main bridge. This bridge was made of iron and carried the road from Peronne to Masnieres, Rumilly and Cambrai; another was a simple wooden edifice. An attempt had been made by the Germans to destroy the main bridge; a tank had tried to get across the damaged structure, but its weight collapsed the bridge. As the tank slid into the canal its crew managed to escape from the hatches. Shortly before this took place, men of 4/Worcesters of 88 Brigade, 29th Division, had managed to get two companies across, but they were stopped by heavy machine-gun fire from making any progress. A small element of 11/RB crossed the canal using the wooden bridge and the twisted girders of the main one, but they had to withdraw with some loss. Masnieres was still strongly held; ten tanks of F Battalion, which had continued their progress after supporting the 12th Division attack, arrived to begin shelling the other side of the canal.

Masnieres Bridge was collapsed by the weight of Tank F22, which attempted to cross the canal 20 November 1917. German soldiers above look down on it from a wooden bridge.

Banteux Lock as it is today. The actual structure has hardly changed. (See pages 44 and 100)

Sergeant R Fitzgerald, 2nd Otago Regiment, cleared the wires and fuses of a German mine at this lock, 30th September 1918.

To the right of 59 Brigade 10/RB, after breaking through the Brown Line, headed for the main road and took up position less than a mile from 11/RB. Two thousand yards to the north west of the 10th was 10/KRRC, which moved up in support of 11/RB. They encountered a large body of the enemy in a sunken road in front of Marcoing Copse. After a brief fight some two hundred gave themselves up, but many others were seen running for the canal, in the hope of safety beyond it. 11/RB had also encountered some opposition on their left, from the same small wood, and after a short skirmish a further 150 Germans surrendered.

Tanks from A Battalion had arrived earlier in the morning at the large village of Marcoing. The main railway bridge leading into the village was still intact, but as the leading tank approached its commander saw a German running towards the bridge. Guessing that he was about to blow it up, the Tank Corps officer leapt from his tank, dashed forward and shot the soldier with his pistol [some shot!]. Observing the proceedings, a body of German infantry advanced to the bridge but they were held off by the tank commander's machine and fell back. No attempt was made just yet to cross the canal, but shortly before midday, within the hour, fourteen tanks arrived from the 6th Division, on the left, which had been involved in the attack on Ribecourt and which had included their commander in Hilda.

One of these new arrivals climbed the railway embankment near the intact bridge and fired on a number of the buildings that sheltered the enemy machine gunners and snipers, silencing most of them.

During the morning the first members of the cavalry arrived in the sector as two troops came from 1/1st Northumberland Hussars; they had linked up with 36 Brigade at Le Quennet farm. In their advance they had charged a German field battery, routed its occupants and captured the guns.

Sometime in the evening of the first day 11/RB was withdrawn from the vicinity of Les Rues Vertes. They then moved eastwards and, without any resistance, took two wooden bridges: one leading from the fields to Mon Plaisir Farm and the other at the lock a further nine hundred yards away. They then attempted to enter the village of Crevecoeur, but in the dark were driven off.

The Division had done its job well, clearing the way from the start line later that morning for the advance of the 29th Division, which now faced the formidable task of breaking through the last line of German defences at the Masnieres-Beaurevoir Line. However, the day was not over for these men; all three of the brigades dug in where they were

The 29th Division:

Major-General Sir Beauvoir de Lisle
Order of Battle

86 Brigade:	87 Brigade:	88 Brigade:
(*Brigade-General GRH Cheape*)	(*Brigadier-General CHT Lucas*)	(*Brigadier-General H Nelson*)
2/R Fusiliers	2/SWB	4/Worcesters
1/LF	1/KOSB	1/Essex
16/Middlesex	1/R Inniskilling F	2/Hants
1/R Guernsey LI	1/Border	Newfoundland Regt

Pioneers: 2/Monmouths

With 14 tanks of A Battalion and strong elements of 455 and 497 Field Companies RE (for bridging); to be followed by the Canadian Brigade of 5th Cavalry Division.

waiting for further developments from the 29th Division, who had now managed to get troops across the canal.

The Division had endured a difficult night even before it started over the top on the morning of 20 November. It had to march from an area slightly north of Peronne through Sorel and Fins to Gouzeaucourt, a distance of some seven miles.; it was to go into battle with objectives four miles away later that day. The task, vital to the success of the whole plan, was to pass through the 12th and 20th Divisions and make for the bridges over the St Quentin canal and seize them, securing the far bank. There were ten of these bridges on their front, a number made of wood. With the canal secured, it was to break the Masnieres-Beaurevoir Line to allow the cavalry attack to proceed. The task was formidable, but the 29th, the 'Incomparable 29th' was the sort of formation that could do it, blooded at Gallipoli, the Somme, Arras and Third Ypres. It would attack with all three brigades in line: 88 heading for Masnieres, on the right; 87 Brigade would be on its left; and 86 Brigade would strike almost due north for the bridges at Marcoing.

The Division was to wait below La Vacquerie to allow the two divisions in front time to break the Hindenburg Line and German resistance south and west of the canal. At 10.15 am Major-General Sir Beauvoir de Lisle gave the order to advance.

On the right 1/Essex, with four tanks from A Battalion, soon ran into a German strong point on the north eastern part of Welsh Ridge that had been either missed or bypassed by the 20th Division. Although it was vital to the Brigade's plan that it should not be delayed at Masnieres, it was also essential to remove this threat. The tanks all failed – three were knocked out by German artillery, one because of a mechanical defect. Despite this, 1/Essex overran the position, collecting an encouraging haul of prisoners and guns; but the stronghold had done its job, slowing the momentum of the advance. 4/Worcesters moved through the Essex and at midday passed through the positions of 11/Rifle Brigade, 59 Brigade, 20th Division. Despite accurate and heavy fire from the German defenders on the far side of the canal they managed to get half the battalion over a wooden bridge at the Sugar Factory. However, this achieved they were pinned down by German fire and could make no further forward movement. The nearby iron bridge, on their left, had collapsed earlier under the weight of a tank; the Worcesters were without immediate hope of help.

In and around Les Rues Vertes with men of 59 Brigade were now those of 4/Worcesters who had not been sent over the canal and 1/Essex, who had managed to get clear of the Hindenburg Support Line, and arrived in the early afternoon. At about 2.30 pm, in a persistent drizzle, the Fort Garry Horse, part of the Canadian Cavalry Brigade, appeared on the scene. Additional troops, in the shape of 2/Hants, 88 Brigade's support battalion, had also come up.

The situation was in the balance. The Germans were obviously in strength on the other side of the canal in the Masnieres-Beaurevoir Line and had no intention of retiring from it, secure in the knowledge that the tanks had been prevented from making a crossing.

2/Hants had as their original objective Rumilly, a village to the north, across the canal and up the steep hill, and therefore to the left of the Worcesters. In the light of events on the other side of the canal, however, they moved south of the village and found a lock. They then quickly moved across and took up positions to the right of the Worcesters, who had been subjected to very heavy fire and had seen their commanding officer, Lieutenant-Colonel CS Linton, killed.

The Fort Garry Horse were not over-enthused about standing around in Les Rues Vertes under fire; and they were impatient to get into the action for which they had waited so long. They searched for a way to cross the canal, and with the help of some of the remaining civilians, they cleared debris away from the Lock bridge (so recently used by 2/Hants) and B Squadron went across. There was murky rain, daylight was gradually slipping away, but they hoped to make the move on Rumilly, behind the Masnieres-Beaurevoir Line.

Meanwhile, behind the new line, in the ground between Les Rues

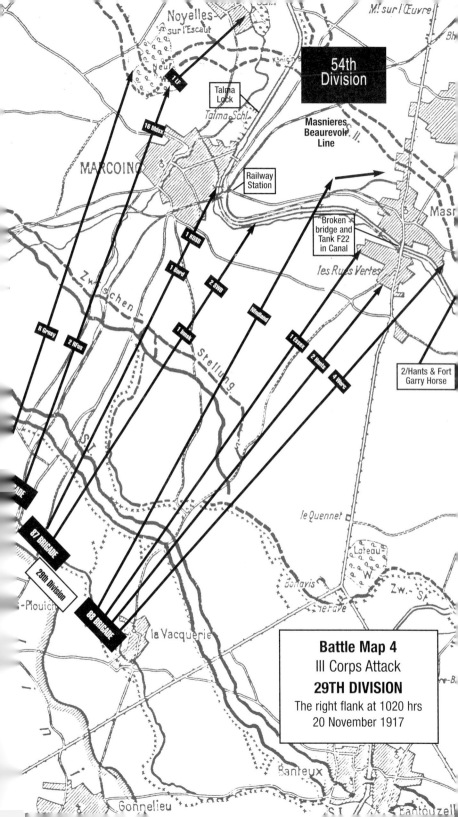

Noyelles
sur l'Escaut

M. sur l'Œuvre

54th
Division

Talma
Lock

Talma-Schl.

19 Mdsx

Masnieres
Beaurevoir
Line

MARCOING

Railway
Station

Mas

Broken
bridge and
Tank F22
in Canal

1 KOSB

1 Bord

les Rues Vertes

2 SWB

R Gensy

2 RFus

1 Innis

Windang

1 Essex

2 Hants

2/Hants & Fort
Garry Horse

4 Worc

le Quennet

87 BRIGADE

29th Division

Bonavis

Lateau
W.

Zw.-SA

Plouich

88 BRIGADE

la Vacquerie

Terave

Battle Map 4
III Corps Attack
29TH DIVISION
The right flank at 1020 hrs
20 November 1917

Gonnelieu

Banteux

Zw. S

Vertes and La Vacquerie, a great bulk of cavalry and the artillery were drawn up waiting for their chance. But it was clear to the cavalry commanders that they could not proceed in force through Masnieres - or anywhere else - for the time being, so their men were told to bivouac for the night and wait for events.

The Fort Garry Horse was on the move, however, and the runners sent to tell them to withdraw failed to arrive. B Squadron found a gap in the German wire and went through it at a gallop, up the hill and into the German defensive line. As was to be expected, German machine-guns took their toll, and the CO of the Squadron, Captain Duncan Campbell, was killed almost immediately. The charge still achieved what the men knew it could do, causing panic and dislocation amongst the German infantry, many of whom were cut down, whilst artillery positions were overrun. However forty Canadians were lying either dead or wounded, and the gloom was rapidly turning to the darkness of an early winter's evening. The remaining troopers took cover in the sunken road running down to Crevecoeur.

The Second in Command was Lieutenant H Strachan, who now organised the Squadron's defence against the enemy, who realised that the rush was over and set about restoring their own situation. The Canadians held them off whilst Strachan decided how to effect an escape from their untenable position. He gave orders to disperse the remaining horses and so distracted the Germans and then, in a fighting withdrawal, brought the remnants of his command back to safety, assisted by the cover provided by the dark, over the canal. He was awarded the Victoria Cross, saw service in the Second World War and lived to a very old age.

Whilst all this had been going on, the Newfoundland Regiment had made its way, not without incident, to the canal to the west of Les Rues Vertes. Their designated wooden bridge on the west side of the village was intact, so the battalion crossed the canal and headed for the German line, with their sights on Rumilly, not quite a mile away to the north east. It was obvious that a penetration of the Masnieres-Beaurevoir Line could not yet be made, not least as its defending wire was uncut and it appeared to be manned in strength, so the Battalion dug in and awaited events. 1/Essex had been struggling to get across, for the bridges in front and to the east of Masnieres were so well covered by machine-guns that no progress could be made, and the artillery had not yet come into action against them.

By midnight on the first day in the right sector of 29th Division, most of 88 Brigade was across the canal: the Newfoundlanders were to the west of Masnieres and 2/Hants, 4/Worcesters and a company of 1/Essex were either in the village trying to clear it or to its east. The fighting continued during the night and in the rain, and by dawn the enemy had, at last, been evicted from the place.

87 Brigade had been led into the attack by 2/SWB, with 1/KOSB on their left, up the Couillet Valley and preceded by four tanks. They followed the main road to Marcoing, passing through Good Old Man Farm, once a German strong point but now evacuated and passed over barbed wire and abandoned German trenches, arriving in the village in good time. Six hundred yards to the rear were 1/RI Fusiliers and to its left 1/Border, 2/SWB and 1/KOSB were to seize the crossings and form bridgeheads in and around Marcoing. This would allow the two following battalions to cross the canal, take the German line and go forward about a mile to Flot Farm, where the canal bends sharply from the south, just to the east of Noyelles.

9/Suffolks of the 6th Division (71 Brigade) had arrived at Marcoing by midday and had cleared that side of it after street fighting in and amongst the houses. When 1/KOSB arrived in the early afternoon there was only the odd small party of the enemy left, and these were soon settled. Then one company crossed the canal by way of the railway bridge whilst a second went over by way of the lock, and advanced on the railway station, a few hundred yards away.

At this stage there were no tanks on the far side, and the remainder of the KOSB pushed into the village, searching for any of the enemy. As soon as 1/Border, coming up behind the leading battalion, saw it had got over the canal, it proceeded to put two companies over, also using the railway bridge and the lock. They were surprised by a lone German machine-gun post, sited on the station platform, that had somehow been missed and which now prevented their advance. Sergeant CE Spackman, without hesitation, went forward alone across open ground. He killed the gunner with his first shot and shot another member of the crew, bayoneted a third before he could get away and captured the gun. He was awarded the Victoria Cross; he survived the war and died in 1969.

Sergeant CE Spackman

1/KOSB by this time had managed to work their way around to both sides of the station, but their eagerness to take it was thwarted by a number of the enemy well entrenched on rising ground to the right.

Cavalry were not used as had been planned, but they were highly mobile and were trained to operate as mounted infantry. They did therefore play an important part in operations at Cambrai.

The march of 2/SWB to Marcoing had been almost uneventful until they came to a small copse almost alongside the canal. In amongst the few trees were a number of snipers whose fire slowed the Welshmen down. Having removed this problem they were further attacked from the far side of the canal by machine-gun fire. As luck would have it however, a tank arrived and with its help in subduing the enemy, three companies got across at the lock. The battalion's right flank was now in touch with that of the Newfoundlanders of 88 Brigade.

During this time two tanks had gone over the main railway bridge and moved northwards for about a mile; they then set about attacking Flot Farm and the surrounding trenches, killing many Germans.

Progress in this area meant that the cavalry could begin their advance. At 2 pm 7/DG (Dragoon Guards) of the Secunderabad Brigade of the 5th Cavalry Division crossed the main bridge and rode to the railway station. They soon came under machine-gun fire and had no option but to dismount and add their support to 1/Border, still held up themselves. In the middle of the afternoon 1/RI Fusiliers, having followed the Welshmen over the canal, advanced on the entrenched Germans who had been holding up 1/KOSB. They were now at the front of the Masnieres-Beaurevoir Line, where the barbed wire was still intact. They launched into an attack and overran the front line of the German defences, killing a great number and forcing more than fifty to surrender as well as capturing a number of machine-guns. The battalion had been led from the front by their commanding officer, Lieutenant-Colonel J, Sherwood-Kelly, armed with his walking stick and a pistol; for his work that day he won the VC, and was to survive the war.

They now attempted to move further forward, but were brought to a halt when they tried to move into the main bulk of the German defence line. Strong resistance made it quite clear that no progress could be made until artillery support was available. To their left rear came 1/Border. There were no tanks and it was getting dark, so the two battalions dug in where they were, only a hundred and fifty yards or so short of their objective; and they awaited further orders. Indeed a company of 1/Border had gone as far forward as Flot Farm, in the wake of the two tanks, but had to withdraw (bringing some prisoners with them) to avoid being cut off.

Lieutenant-Colonel J, Sherwood-Kelly

At about 4 pm 5/DG arrived from the 1st Cavalry Division, with orders to advance east of the canal and take Noyelles. A squadron of the Dragoons went over the canal at the main railway bridge, hoping to get to Flot Farm, but it was now dark and the farm was still in enemy hands. They returned to the other side of the canal, saddled up, to wait for events.

The third, left, brigade of the 29th Division, 86, had started its advance by marching up the Couillet valley, sheltered on its left by the long wood covering the steep slope. It had the task of taking the two lines of German trenches, an extension of the Masnieres-Beaurevoir Line, that crossed the canal at Flot Farm and went through Nine Wood, a mile to the west. 16/Middlesex led the way, with four tanks of A Battalion. When they arrived at the wood shortly before midday they found a number of tanks waiting for them from H Battalion (minus their commander, Elles, whose tank had been knocked out at the Grand Ravin on the edge of Ribecourt). The defenders put up little resistance and Nine Wood was soon under the control of 16/Middlesex.

On the left 1/RGLI (Royal Guernsey Light Infantry) was now to go into action for the first time. The men had arrived from England only four weeks earlier to join 86 Brigade; they went to the north west corner of Nine Wood to ensure it was clear of the enemy before taking up positions looking north to Noyelles and west facing Premy Chapel. The battalion was just a few hundred yards on the right of troops of the 6th Division.

With the British safely removed from the battlefield, this German could afford to take a relaxed pose beside this disabled tank.

Chapter Three

21 – 27 NOVEMBER 1917

21st November 1917

By the early hours of the 22nd 2/Hants and 4/Worcs had finally cleared the enemy out of Masnieres and had advanced two hundred yards up the road towards Rumilly. 1/Essex had crossed the lock to the west of the village and had advanced as far as the railway line three hundred yards north of the canal. It was raining heavily; by first light a patrol of 4/Worcesters had met men of 11/RB from the 20th Division. To the front left of 86 Brigade, at the south west corner of Noyelles, a dismounted troop of 18/Hussars relieved the squadron of 4/DG.

Third Army's order for the 21st instructed de Lisle and Douglas Smith to arrange their own Zero hour for their combined operation that morning; they decided that, after a heavy barrage by the artillery, this would be at 11 am for the three brigades of the 29th Division and 59 Brigade of the 20th.

10/RB was to facilitate the advance across the canal by attempting to cross it at a point where it makes a sharp U bend between Crevecoeur and Les Rues des Vignes. At 6.30 am the battalion attacked Les Rues des Vignes, but found that it was impossible to cross the lock to the east of the church because of the German machine-guns beyond it. At the northern end of the village the German presence on the western side of the canal could not be overcome. A company was left at the lock and two other companies withdrew back up the valley slopes.

Before the main attack could commence, the Germans made their first counter strike against the 29th Division; at 10.30 am the Germans attacked 86 Brigade, which was in part of the outer edge of the Masnieres-Beaurevoir Line at Noyelles and which they reckoned posed the most immediate threat. Lines of men were seen by the Hampshires and Worcesters advancing from behind their line out of Crevecoeur and towards Mon Plaisir Farm. Despite heavy fire from the British infantry and a barrage from the field artillery, the Germans pressed on towards the north west. Within an hour 86 Brigade was under attack. Shortly after midday 2/RF, two platoons of 1/LF and the thirty troopers of 8/Hussars found they could no longer keep the enemy out of the village. Fighting continued into the afternoon, the Germans unable to make any further gains, despite receiving reinforcements. Reinforcements from 9/Lancers saved the day by holding the wooden bridge over the river at the chateau. At 4 pm two tanks arrived and with 2/RF and 18/Hussars restored full control of the village, However the Germans still remained in the vicinity on its northern and western sides. Later in the afternoon another squadron of 9/Lancers was sent into the village and took up position with other elements of the regiment in the chateau grounds.

16/Middlesex fought all afternoon and by dusk took possession of enemy trenches at a junction on the Cantaing road. The R Guernsey LI, on the left flank of the Brigade all day in their positions in Nine Wood, held off German patrols coming from the north. After dark on the 21st the brigade was relieved at Noyelles by the 6th Division and moved into billets in Marcoing.

87 Brigade was to cross the canal, take Flot Farm and thereby break through the Masnieres-Beaurevoir Line south east of Noyelles. The assault was to be led by 2/SWB and 1/KOSB with the assistance of thirty tanks. The attack was delayed by an hour because there was only the one iron bridge at Marcoing by which these mechanical monsters could cross. For some reason the tanks did not go forward to crush the enemy wire for the lead battalions, but rather cruised up and down the German lines, blazing away at the German defenders, with very limited success. The infantry, delayed by the tanks, were further frustrated by being confronted by uncut wire and could do little. The Welsh managed to get into some houses and held them for a while against German counter attacks; but 1/Essex were held up on the Masnieres road as they came up to offer support, and by dusk the British were back on their start line. The tanks also suffered, badly mauled by German field guns firing at close range and by heavy machine-gun and rifle fire using armour-piercing bullets. In fact only three were knocked out and lost, but the rest were badly damaged, their armour plate pierced in many places. One tank commander reported thirty seven holes in his machine; and some were set on fire. There were, not surprisingly, a large number of Tank Corps casualties. 87 Brigade's attack was over.

88 Brigade, not surprisingly, was exhausted after its exertion before the Masnieres-Beaurevoir Line at Masnieres. The objective set for it on the 21st was the capture of two thousand yards of the German line from the Cambrai road eastwards to Crevecoeur, and there join with 59 Brigade. However the 88th was too tired and depleted to do the job. All that Brigadier-General Nelson could do was to consolidate his position. He put 1/Essex and 2/Hants on the defensive facing the Masnieres-Beaurevoir Line in front of Masnieres; the Newfoundland

Explosion and fire in a confined metal transporter – the effects of a direct hit on a tank. The crew's desperate attempts to get out are only too evident.
TAYLOR LIBRARY

Regiment, which was at the Sugar Factory during the day, went under cover in the houses for the night.

At 11 am 59 Brigade's attack was due to begin; 11/KRRC would lead, passing through 11/RB, which had been there all night in front of Crevecoeur. The battalion was expecting to have tanks with it, but they still had not arrived at 1 pm. Without waiting any longer, at 1.20 pm, 11/KRRC set off, but soon came under rifle fire and was enfiladed from the Masnieres-Beaurevoir Line. A company was then sent across the lock and the battalion turned left to face the enemy fire coming from Crevecoeur. At 3 pm four tanks approached down the hill from Revelon Chateau, high on the west bank. The enemy at the bridge fled from their fire, but it was getting dark and the tank commanders were unconvinced that the bridge would take the weight of their machines; consequently they withdrew to the chateau grounds. 11/KRRC, deprived of the tanks' fire support, withdrew in its entirety with them. A mile to the south in Les Rues des Vignes, 10/RB, who had charged into the village as it became dark to get in touch with 11/KRRC at the lock, also withdrew.

On the second day the audacious plan to swoop over the St Quentin canal in a right hook for Cambrai had faltered again, and then come to

Ruined church at Marcoing.

a halt. De Lisle, in his headquarters outside Gouzeaucourt, in the Quentin Mill, at least seven miles as the crow flies from the front, reported that his Division was now unfit for any attack on the German line without a heavy preparatory bombardment and twenty tanks.

That evening Haig closed down the operation on the right. The right hook and the taking of Rumilly was no longer on the cards; the bridges at Crevecoeur had been beyond the capabilities of the 20th and 29th Divisions. The grand plan of a mass of cavalry charging across the canal at Crevecoeur going for Niergnies and Awoingt was over. All efforts from now on were to be directed at Bourlon Ridge, to menace the Germans east of Arras and to cut off Cambrai from the west. The three southern divisions would consolidate the defensive flank at the canal and no further advances would be made. He would permit the Bourlon operation to continue for another forty eight hours.

The 12th Division front would extend north easterly from the Banteux Ravine, east of the road along the Bonavis Ridge up to and including Lateau Wood and with observation over the canal valley. On 24 November limited operations were carried out to improve the position: 5/Berks attacked and secured Quarry Post and 8/R Fusiliers attacked the long Pelican Trench, north west of Banteux, capturing part of it.

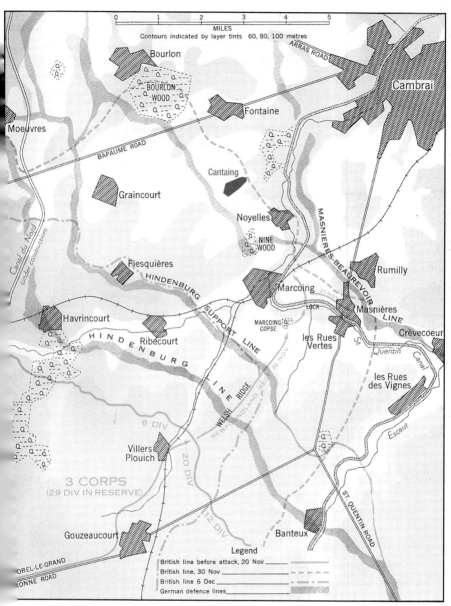

A layered map of the Cambrai battlefield showing the main topographical features and the changing fortunes of the battle. It should be used in conjunction with the earlier battle maps and the area map on page 12.

The 20th Division held the line from the Cambrai road beyond Lateux Wood down to the St Quentin canal, holding posts opposite Crevecoeur.

29th Division held the part of the Masnieres-Beaurevoir Line that they had captured, the spur west of Rumilly to the lock at Marcoing railway station. The line then went from the west side of the canal to join with the 6th Division west of Noyelles.

The three divisions would convert the Hindenburg Second Line behind them into a second defence line. The 29th was ordered to try and push forward to Rumilly, which they attempted so to do on the 23rd but failed owing to the weight of enemy fire, None of the divisions were relieved and, as they had not received any reinforcements, they were now much reduced by being in action for so long and in such terrible weather.

Rupprecht was unable to launch a counter attack at this stage, though he was aware that the attacks at Masnieres had ceased and that fresh preparations were being made before Bourlon Wood. Reinforcements were coming in at a rapid rate and he had been promised four more divisions by Ludendorff. He reckoned that he would have to hold on for two or three more days of considerable attack, by which time the British infantry would be exhausted and the tanks should practically have disappeared from the battlefield. His target date for a massive counter attack to regain all that he had lost had to be between 27 - 30 November, before the winter snows stopped everything.

22 – 27 November

The remaining days of the battle centred on the fight for Bourlon and Bourlon Wood. It is no part of this book to describe events here; attacks by the 40th Division and the Guards Division (the latter fighting in driving snow) failed to secure the desired objectives, and all efforts were instead concentrated on retaining a hold on the western part of the wood and the high ridge. The offensive against Cambrai was halted and preparations were set in train to face the German counter offensive.

Chapter Four

THE GERMAN COUNTER OFFENSIVE: 30 NOVEMBER – 7 DECEMBER 1917

The Plan

Crown Prince Rupprecht and Ludendorff met at the headquarters of the Second Army at Le Cateau on 27 November. The proposal was that the British would be rolled up towards the north. The attack would be in the general direction of Metz, capturing Flesquieres and Havrincourt Wood from the south, the idea being to take the British from flank and rear. Once this attack was well established there would be another thrust, southwards, by all the forces available from the west of Bourlon Wood. The idea was, therefore, an uppercut from below to be followed by a hammer blow on top. If all this went well, further attacks could be envisaged further south, in the vicinity of St Quentin.

The German assault started with a massive barrage of gas shells into Bourlon Wood on 28 November. Meanwhile more German troops were arriving, notably a couple of divisions which were released from Flanders, the provision of which had encouraged Ludendorff to consider such a wide ranging counter stroke. Of course, the one thing that the Germans did not have was tanks.

Crown Prince Rupprecht

Friday 30th November

The British held a salient nine miles wide and four deep, in ground which was not particularly easy to defend. All the troops were very tired and there were few tanks left, although 48 new ones had arrived at Metz on the 28th. The British also sent in a number of fresher divisions - the 55th had been on the right flank of the 12th Division for some time, in the Villers Guislain area; the 37th was brought into support of the 12th; the 2nd was further north, up near Bourlon; the 59th (North Midland) was to relieve the Guards near Fontaine; the 47th (2/London) was to take the 62nd's place north of Graincourt whilst the 6th Division put its 16 Brigade at Ribecourt, towards Gouzeaucourt.

Both VII Corps commander (Snow) and the 55th Division commander (Jeudwine) were well aware of the build-up of German forces opposite them and what it presaged. The front that the 55th held was very lengthy, nine thousand yards, something which might usually be held by three divisions. In the north it was adjacent, at an awkward, almost right angle, to the 12th Division; and the line then ran down in front of Villers Guislain to Lempire, about three miles north of Epehy. The Division was also very short of artillery support. On the positive side the weather had cleared sufficiently for the RFC to give a good idea of what the Germans were doing.

The cavalry, whose moment of glory had never come, had elements now acting in a dismounted role, and some were concentrated west of Gouzeaucourt.

30 November dawned misty, following a fine night. A desultory German bombardment began at 6 am, but quickly grew in intensity, a mixture of gas and high explosive.

At 7 am the advance began against 165 Brigade, in its positions east of Lempire, and 166 Brigade, in its positions west of Banteux running to the south east of Villers Guislain. The Germans overran a company of 1/5 S Lancs in front of Villers Guislain, and pushed on towards the divisional boundary with the 12th Division and 35 Brigade just beyond its north western edge.

As yet the southern part of the 20th Division was relatively unaffected by proceedings, but from 7 am heavy machine-gun and artillery fire fell on 86 Brigade (29th Division) at Masnieres, on 87 Brigade at Marcoing and 61 Brigade, the northern part of 20th Division, at Les Rues Vertes. The three divisions had been transformed from exultant conquerors to desperate defenders in a matter of days.

The 55th Division faced four German divisions as it strove to thwart Ludendorff's plan to roll up the British salient with a swift, lethal uppercut blow. It had had to fall back almost four thousand yards and lost Villers Guislain, but it had acted as a sturdy anchor in holding the basis of the British position steady.

German troops at La Vacquerie in 1918. An obviously posed photograph, showing the alertness, keeness and professionalism of the German soldier, it would have been used extensively for propaganda purposes.

The 12th Division's Story.

The advance by the Germans on the right flank of 35 Brigade gave them an ideal point from which to attack the three thousand yard position the Brigade held before Gonnelieu. The commander, Brigadier-General B Vincent, had his headquarters in a dugout near a cemetery, half a mile north west of Villers Guislain on the road to Gouzeaucourt. The preliminary German bombardment had broken all his signal wires connecting him to the forward elements of his brigade, some two thousand yards to the north west, and with the neighbouring 166 Brigade of the 55th Division. He was completely surprised to find the Germans in the village at 7.30 am, and proceeded to pull together a composite force before beating a hasty retreat. Along with his staff he had some Royal Engineers of the 69th Field Company and a Vickers machine-gun and crew from the 235th Machine Gun Company. Harassed by enemy shell fire and low flying aircraft machine-guns, he fought a withdrawal to the west, heading for the relative shelter of

Gauche Wood, halfway between Villers Guislain and Gouzeaucourt. He now had a complement of about a hundred men, having gathered in stragglers and lost survivors from the tide of the German advance. The wood was now a target for the German artillery, being both a wood (and therefore a natural point for shelter in the open landscape) and occupying a prominent position in the landscape. The force was now withdrawn a few hundred yards further to the west, to the relative security of a railway cutting and embankment. From here his men put up a sustained rate of rifle fire, deterring the enemy from leaving the wood in pursuit. Like the British before them, the Germans were also beginning to outrun their guns' ability to provide effective fire support. In due course Vincent withdrew again, looking for higher ground five hundred yards below Gouzeaucourt. His small band had been diminished still further, but he was able to divert two battalions. 11/Middlesex and 6/Queen's, who were in the process of joining their respective brigades, the 36th and 37th, as they faced their own assault from the Germans. Gonnelieu, two miles to the north west, had also fallen to the German's 34th Division; a company of 5/Northamptons, the divisional pioneers, had withdrawn from there and were added to Vincent's force. He also managed to add three more machine-guns from 235 Machine Gun Company. From a small ragbag of men his force had grown into a significant battle field presence.

Gonnelieu had been heavily shelled from the outset of the German attack; by 7.30 am all communications to and from it had been broken. It faced an attack from the 34th German Division coming from the Banteux Ravine. In the village were the headquarters of 36 Brigade under Brigadier-General CS Owen and an assortment of Royal Engineers, 5/Northamptons and the headquarters of five artillery batteries. South east of the village were 7/Suffolks of 35 Brigade. Just behind the village, in a long trench between it and the road (Green Switch and Gin Avenue), were the 70th Field Company, RE and two companies of the Northamptons. These were joined by some gunners from the 354th Siege Battery.

To avoid being overrun, the headquarters of 36 Brigade moved back down the valley into Villers Plouich soon after fighting began; Owen simply had no time to organise a defence of Gonnelieu. Also in Villers Plouich was the headquarters of 37 Brigade.

7/Suffolks had been shelled with gas and high explosive from the beginning of the German offensive, and had come under attack not only from the front but also from the rear. The battalion was virtually wiped out, their commander, Major GH Henty, and most of his eighteen officers either killed or wounded. The Germans could not claim the village as theirs whilst the British artillery pulversised them. Four batteries played havoc on them at short range, although at terrible cost to the gunners. C/63 Battery was reduced to two guns and six men, for example. Stripping the guns of their sights and breech blocks, their commander, Lieutenant Wallace, and his tiny band withdrew. Wallace won the VC (he survived the war and went on to serve in the RAF in the Second World War) and the five surviving men gained the DCM.

Lieutenant Wallace

35 Brigade was now split by a distance of some three thousand yards, with its commander way down to the right, near Gouzeaucourt. Gonnelieu had almost fallen and 7/Suffolks had ceased to exist as a fighting force. To the north east of the village, near The Barricade and Sonnet Farm, were 5/Berks and 9/Essex; to their left rear, near Bleak House, was the fourth battalion of the Brigade, 7/Norfolks.

5/Berks' advanced platoon at Quarry Post was the first to be attacked, by the 109th Grenadiers, and the whole battalion had to give

Gonnelieu, 1917 after the Germans had captured it in their counter-offensive 30 November 1917.

Elements of the German 34th Division came down this street towards the camera

Battalion Grenadier Guards entered age 1st December, but were driven out h heavy casualties – ten officers, 195 et ranks. Captain Paton won the VC. e page 84)

After the battle: German soldiers examine the remains of a British howitzer gun position after a direct hit.

ground; at 10.30 am it was forced to retire to the ridge, close to the main road. The Essex, already on top of the ridge, along with the Berkshires, fought to stop the Germans, who were assisted by artillery and low flying aircraft. In the early afternoon both battalions were pushed back over the road into the old German defences at La Vacquerie. At about 8 am it was the turn of 7/Norfolks to come under direct attack. Their position was enormously strengthened by seven of the machine-guns of the 35th Machine Gun Company, but in the end they were overwhelmed and with heavy losses. Amongst those killed was their commanding officer, Lieutenant Colonel HLFA Gielgud. However, the Germans were still unable to get across the road.

Whilst 35 Brigade was being attacked piece meal, with command coming from the highest ranking officer on the spot, 36 Brigade was facing a similar situation. 8 and 9/R Fusiliers were the front battalions holding positions on the road between Bleak House and Le Pave on the Bonavis Ridge; the 9th was joined by a small group of survivors from 7/Norfolks in Pelican Trench.

The German attack by 190 Reserve Regiment was far too strong for the depleted Brigade to hold, and the men withdrew into the defences around La Vacquerie; in the process a number of men of 9/R Fusiliers were taken prisoner when Bleak House fell. 8/R Fusiliers, holding a position on both sides of the road, were in a desperate situation by mid-morning. The two leading companies were crushed by the enemy attacks, and attempts to reinforce them by a third company were met with sustained machine-gun fire which left them stranded on open ground. The Commanding Officer, Lieutenant-Colonel NB Elliott-Cooper, gathered his Headquarters staff and his remaining company and charged over the main road, pushing the enemy beyond the crest. With this respite, it was possible to gather the residue of the battalion and withdraw to La Vacquerie and there join with 7/Suffolks. With eleven machine-guns from the 36th Machine Gun Company, a defensive line facing east was established. Elliott-Cooper's charge had been truly heroic – and, perhaps more to the point,

Lieutenant-Colonel NB Elliott-Cooper,

successful. However, he was severely wounded in the attack; he was sufficiently aware to order the withdrawal to La Vacquerie, but he was to die of his wounds three months later, when he was a Prisoner of War. This gallant officer had already won the DSO and MC; to this was to be added the VC. He is buried in Hamburg.

37 Brigade was arranged around Bonavis and Pam Pam farms; 7/E Surreys occupied both buildings (or, rather, their remnants) with 6/E Kents behind. To the left, at Lateau Wood, was 6/RWK, whilst the fourth battalion of the Brigade was, literally, miles away, to the south west of Gouzeaucourt, incorporated into Vincent's force. Brigadier-General Incledon-Webber's three battalions were going to have one very memorable day.

The German forces coming up to the attack were men of the 55th and 99th Regiment, 220th Division. These set about enveloping 7/E Surrey's from the east, and by 8.30 am that position had been so compromised that Brigade Headquarters was forced to defend itself, driving off an attack. Things were made worse when the Germans threatened Pam Pam Farm, behind their right flank; suffering from the enemy bombardment as well, they fell back into the old Hindenburg Line trenches and were there reinforced by a company from 6/E Kents. From this position they launched a counter attack and pushed the

Germans back over the road; they then consolidated by occupying a trench that ran alongside it. There was to be no respite, least of all from the artillery of both sides. Such was the state of confusion about the location of the line, the poor defenders had to accept shell fire from both German and British guns. Once more the battalion retired, but this time further than before, as by now the Germans had taken full control of Pam Pam Farm. A further blow was the capture of their Commanding Officer, Lieutenant-Colonel RH Baldwin.

6/RWK, in Lateau Wood, had also come under fierce attack, especially from the north east, where the Brigade touched the outposts of 59 Brigade at Le Quennet Farm. By 11 am the West Kents (whose quite extraordinary commander, Lieutenant-Colonel WRA Dawson, was to win the DSO four times, had been wounded early in the day) were driven out of their posts and men of the German 190th Regiment were in the farm. As the Germans advanced over the Bonavis Ridge, so survivors of 37 Brigade, men of 6/Buffs (East Kents), a few East Surreys and West Kents, a few gunners and the eight machine-guns from the 37th Machine Gun Company defended their position in the Hindenburg Line under the command of Lieutenant-Colonel AS Smeltzer of the Buffs. They could not hold on for long, as the enemy attack from the north was too strong. Gradually they made a fighting withdrawal deeper into the old German defences, helped by 179 Brigade RFA firing over open sights at the closing enemy. Many from the gun crews were killed.

Before it became dark, at around 4 pm, Smeltzer's force connected with the remnants of 36 Brigade and held a line in front of La Vacquerie, where the German attacks finally ceased. The casualties in men, artillery and machine-guns had been heavy; for example, out of one detachment of eight guns from the 235th Machine Gun Company only three men survived in the British lines.

The 12th Division's left flank, forced back to La Vacquerie, had not collapsed despite the weight of attacks upon it; but the few survivors had been fought to their physical limit. The Germans, however, had far from being having things their own way. They had been surprised by the obstinacy of the resistance and had suffered very heavy losses. Their hopes of storming over the main road, retaking La Vacquerie and the Hindenburg Line positions and then moving on to Metz en Couture, had been effectively thwarted.

Down in the south, separated from his troops, Vincent had established a line along the Revelon Ridge; 11/Middlesex held the northern part, down to Chapel Hill and 6/Queen's held the line down

British artillerymen manhandle their gun to engage a new target. The scale of their fire task is indicated by the large stack of prepared ordnance.

to Vaucelette Farm. Although too weak to act offensively, the force acted as a garrison for the reserve line, whilst cavalry (dismounted) came forward. The Guards Division towards the end of the day recaptured Gouzeaucourt, which had been lost earlier.

The 20th (Light) Division's Story

On the morning of 30 November the Divisional front was held by two brigades, the 59th (which after seven days in reserve had just relieved the 60th) on the right and the 61st on the left. By this time none of the battalions had a fighting strength over 400; some of them were well under 300. Command confusion promised to be great, as the relief of the 60th by the 59th Brigade Headquarters was not complete before the German attack commenced. Brigadier-General Duncan (GOC 60 Brigade) therefore commanded the 59th throughout the operation; whilst the temporary commander of 59 Brigade (the GOC being away) Lieutenant-Colonel Troyte-Bullock took control of 60 Brigade, which was either in, or making its way to, Villers Plouich, the Brigade reserve area. This confusion in commanders meant that in some cases they did not even know the unit commanders in their temporary commands,

The story of 60 Brigade does not really belong to that of the 20th

Division on this day. Major-General Douglas Smith was unaware as late as 9 am that the German assault to the south would involve his front; therefore his reserve Brigade, so opportunely positioned, was used to reinforce the deteriorating position of the 12th Division. Indeed, within some minutes after 9 am, it was clear that Villers Plouich itself was threatened. 60 Brigade now moved to defensive positions: 6/KSLI, at the time in Villers Plouich, moved southwards towards Gouzeaucourt, taking positions around the Quarry, the main road to Cambrai and the station. The Ox and Bucks, who were coming into Villers Plouich after their relief, was sent off to take position to the left of the KSLI, on the ridge to the north of Gonnelieu. It was about this time that Lieutenant Wallace and his men were fighting the desperate action that was to bring them a raft of decorations. 12/RB was ordered to assist 35 Brigade, by now almost overwhelmed, whilst the last battalion in the reserve brigade, 12/KRRC, moved to La Vacquerie, to aid with the defence of that vital position. In all of this it needs to be borne in mind that, although this was nominally the reserve brigade, the men were exhausted from their time in the front (and the asssault), and had also endured a march to the reserve line after some days of sedentary warfare, before being unexpectedly moved off to a completely new part of the front. 20th Division's reserve in Villers Plouich now consisted solely of the pioneers, 11/DLI.

If Douglas Smith thought things difficult on the right, his two weak brigades on his front proper were going to face a real test as they faced an attack by two German divisions. Their position on the Bonavis Ridge was hazardous. They were overlooked from the high ground on the far side of the St Quentin canal at Crevecoeur and Vaucelles; yet they were unable to view the canal itself because of the steep fall of the ground into the valley below. To the north the 29th Division was vulnerable to a German attack over the canal, and there was the possibility of a breakthrough to the north of that Division's front which would leave both of them open to an attack from the rear. The outpost line down the slope into the marshy ground of the valley was long, weakly held and inadequately wired. There had been no time (or men) to dig the necessary communication trenches and, as already noted, he had no reserve brigade.

The mist was particularly thick in the area around Lateau Wood, just beyond the left of 59 Brigade front; the situation for the defenders was extremely confusing, due to the fact that they found themselves under attack not only from their front but also from their right and right rear. The German infantry advanced in a succession of from eight to

A Lewis gun positioned for anti-aircraft work. The soldiers have used a post as a makeshift mounting and made full use of the felled tree to provide cover.

twelve waves, preceded (where conditions allowed) by a great number of low-flying aircraft which poured machine-gun fire on the defenders and dropped smoke bombs, as necessary, to cover the advance of the troops. Thus it was that 10/KRRC and, to its left, 11/KRRC found themselves confronted with swarms of infantry from the 220th Division emerging from the mist. With no time to fall back or reorganise, the two battalions battled it out; by the end of the day only four officers and sixteen men of 10/KRRC were on their feet, having managed to work their way back to La Vacquerie.

Five hundred yards to the rear of the two battalions was 10/RB; they could hear the sound of the battle before them, but could see nothing of it. They were quickly attacked and overwhelmed; indeed the Commanding Officer, Lieutenant-Colonel LHW Troughton, was captured whilst on the telephone reporting the battle 'in front of him'. Some of those that managed to escape and fought their way out of the enemy ring around them, moved to the left into 61 Brigade's sector, joining with their reserve battalion, 7/DCLI. All that remained of 59 Brigade was 11/RB, in reserve in the Hindenburg Line, a thousand yards to the rear at the start of the fighting but a position that was rapidly becoming the front line. This battalion, along with stragglers from the forward battalions and men from overrun gun lines, managed to stabilize the line.

German counter attacks

German fighter plane forced down on the British side of the line. The aggressive role played by the German airforce was an integral part of the counter-offensive plan.

The artillery had played a formidable role in the defence of the position. Gunners stayed at their posts until the last moment, and even then most had the nouse to take breech blocks and sights with them as they beat their own hasty retreat. Their actions throughout the 30th served to slow the German advance towards La Vacquerie and took a particularly heavy toll of them as they advanced over Bonavis Ridge, to the north of Lateau Wood.

The positions of the battalions of 61 Brigade were equally as weak as those in their neighbouring brigade. Two of the battalions were well forward of the road to Masnieres, on the slope down to Les Rues des Vignes, though this village was not visible to them. To the right was 12/King's with two companies in the outpost line, one at the main road and one near Brigade Headquarters on the eastern slope of La Vacquerie valley; on the left was 7/SLI, with three of its companies well forward. Like their neighbours, the two battalions were overwhelmed by the German attack within some two hours of vicious, close-quarter, fighting. Both the commanding officers were away from their battalions on leave; Major RB Charsley, commanding the King's, was soon missing (in fact killed) and Major RP Preston-Whyte, commanding the Somersets, was seriously wounded.

61 Brigade's support battalion, 7/DCLI, were unprepared for the sudden onrush of the Germans, members of the 30th Division. The Cornwalls' commander (another second in command) was killed

whilst leading a counter attack; whilst the position itself was very vulnerable to enemy strafing from the air, open and treeless as it was. In due time the battalion fell back across the valley to the reserve battalion's (7/KOYLI) position. The KOYLIs held a very large front – on the left they were in touch with 1/KOSB of the 29th Division, just below Marcoing, and on the right they were in contact with the tattered remnants of 59 Brigade. They had as their left flank guard two companies of the Divisional Pioneers, 11/DLI, and with the various other flotsam of the Brigade, managed to hold the line on Welsh Ridge. The thrust of the overwhelming German attack succeeded in its attempt to drive west across the valley to Couillet Wood.

60 Brigade, to the south, was not idle as the day progressed. At 2 pm the Ox and Bucks launched an attack over the main road to Cambrai up Quentin Ridge. They were halted by German fire, but managed to get into Gin Avenue, a long trench north of Gonnelieu; it was here that 12/RB had been sent earlier in the day to help the battered battalions of 35 Brigade. At Gouzeaucourt there was now a great melee of men from different brigades and divisions. Close by 6/KSLI were 4/Grenadiers of the Guards Division. A warning order was given to the three battalions of 60 Brigade in the vicinity that they were to take part in an operation that night. The weather had improved and 30 November was a fine night. 6/KSLI, after a hasty reconnaissance, moved out of its position in the Quarry, followed the railway line south and then turned to the east to attack the Germans entrenched on Quentin Ridge – the target of the failed attack by 6/Ox and Bucks. They too failed, but did manage to occupy a trench close to Green Street; simultaneous with this attack the Ox and Bucks and 12/RB tried to enter Gonnelieu, but had no great success. The Shropshires were removed after their failure and replaced by men of 16 Brigade (6th Division) who were to have another go immediately at capturing the position; but this too failed, not helped by the fact that the men involved were completely new to the ground.

At the end of 30 November 60 Brigade was the only formation in the 20th (Light) Division fit to carry out offensive operations in the following days.

The 29th Division on the 30th November.

This was to be one of those rare battles where the divisional commander had almost as hair-raising a day as those of his men in the front line. Indeed, it was reported that Major-General Beauvoir de Lisle had to make an escape in his pyjamas, though he actually had been up for some time, had breakfast and was en route to visit the front. His Headquarters were at the old Quentin Mill on the edge of Gouzeaucourt. At 8.45 am, with the German attack on the 55th Division heading towards them, but still some distance away, the mill came under artillery and machine-gun fire. Within minutes, as the German infantry came pouring over Quentin Ridge, it became clear that the position was in imminent danger of being captured. The BGRA, Brigadier-General EH Stevenson, had already been severely wounded and could not be moved. Left behind with a wounded orderly, he was captured by the Germans, but was liberated during the counter attack of 1 December. The General and his staff left the hill top mill in a hurry, the short defence being left to a few men in Headquarters, pioneers and sappers, and a detachment – surprisingly enough US Engineers from the 11th (Railway) Detachment. They suffered, if not the first, amongst the earliest US losses, with one officer and twenty seven men casualties, a number of them taken prisoner.

The Divisional front lay on the German side of the St Quentin canal; 86 Brigade covered Masnieres, 87 Brigade Marcoing and 88 Brigade was in reserve, to the left of the 87th.

16/Middlesex was on the extreme right flank of 86 Brigade, with forward platoons in Mon Plaisir Farm, on the main road from Masnieres to Crevecoeur, and at the bridge three hundred yards below the farm. 1/L Fusiliers were on the left, holding the line to the main road from Masnieres to Cambrai. In the village were 2/R Fusiliers, 1/R Guernsey LI and the Headquarters of 86 Brigade. On the southern side of the canal behind them there were no infantry at all, reliance being placed on 61 Brigade.

At 7 am the German attack started with heavy artillery and machine-gun fire on the Brigade's position. By 9 am the German attack began with a movement of infantry out of the Masnieres-Beaurevoir Line under the protective machine-gun fire of low-flying aircraft. The advance was halted before it reached the British line by rifle fire and the machine-guns of the Brigade's company. However, the Middlesex, on the right, had to give ground. To the south of 86 Brigade (blissfully ignorant) the German 30th Division had broken through 61 Brigade and, with nothing to stop them, were charging towards Les Rues Vertes. Their aim was to by-pass the British on the far side of the canal and cut them off by capturing Marcoing.

In Les Rues Vertes that morning was a section of the 497th (Kent) Field Company RE, asleep at the brewery on the southern edge of the canal after working through the night. Surprised, to put it mildly, by the arrival of the Germans, they were taken prisoner as they woke from sleep and their captors then proceeded up the village street towards the canal bridge.

86 Brigade's rear Headquarters were on the village side of the broken bridge; tank F22 still lying in the water. The Brigade Staff Captain, Captain R Gee, grasped what was taking place five hundred yards away, and was already alerted to the German intentions by his Brigade commander, who was on the other side of the canal. He immediately sent a runner to warn 88 Brigade in Marcoing of events, and began to organise a defence of the bridge with the umpromising material he had available. This consisted of twelve signallers and orderlies of his HQ and Captain CE Loseby of the Lancashire Fusiliers, whose own battalion was on the other side of the canal.

Captain R Gee

Loseby and six of the men were sent across the canal to make contact with 16/Middlesex at the lock bridge. Gee, with the remaining men, took a Lewis gun and their rifles and went into the nearest house. They brought out the furniture to barricade the street. The Germans were astonished, both at the scene and the hail of rifle and machine-gun fire, and fell back. Gee then went to get more ammunition from the brigade stock, kept in another house. There he was pounced upon by two Germans; he killed one with an iron-shod stick and struggled with the other until two of his men came and dealt with his opponent.

By this stage reinforcements, in the shape of forty men from the Guernsey Light Infantry, had arrived over the canal bridge to assist with holding the bridgehead; shortly afterwards two more companies arived. Gee now had a force with which he could take offensive action; he strengthened the barricade and then went forward with a bombing team, driving the enemy back. At the fork in the road, halfway through the village, he built another barricade and then linked up with Captain Loseby's position at the canal lock.

With this position established he proceeded to work at driving the Germans back down the street; the Germans had had enough, this diversion was costing them time and men which they did not have in abundance, and so they withdrew. However, the Germans were still keen to keep the British trapped, and left a machine-gun behind, dug into the sunken road below the village. This would hold the situation until the manpower could be found to attack again and remove the obstacle of the British held southern bridgehead.

Captain Gee was determined to destroy this German position, Under the protective fire of a small mortar, he and another man charged the gun. His accomplice was killed, but, using two revolvers, he was able to capture the gun. With the assistance of some Guernsey men, who had moved up to the position, he was able to turn the machine-gun around on the enemy and covered an infantry attack which silenced another machine-gun. A bombing party was able to set up another block and thereby secured the entry to the village. Gee was soon afterwards wounded in the knee; but after it was dressed, and secure in the knowledge that the village was relatively safe, he crossed to Brigade Headquarters on the far side. On top of all his other exploits, this extraordinary man was forced to swim the canal to get to the safety of Marcoing when he faced the probability of capture the following morning. Almost needless to say, he was awarded the Victoria Cross for actions which ensured the recapture of the village, and, quite probably, saved the bulk of the 29th Division. This long-serving regular officer of 2/R Fusiliers was too severely wounded to return to the Western Front, serving out the remainder of his war with the Teeside Garrison. He moved to Perth in Australia, where he died many years later, in 1960.

With the situation in the village restored, half 2/R Fusiliers were brought back over the canal to defend the south west of the village. With dusk the attacks on 86 Brigade at Les Rues Vertes came to a halt; Brigadier-General Cheape could rest his men as best he could and prepare for the onslaught that would surely come the following day. The rest was needed; all through the day on the far side of the canal the men of the Middlesex had endured heavy shelling and enfilade fire from machine-guns. Their Commanding Officer, Lieutenant-Colonel J Forbes-Robinson, still visited all parts of his battalion despite the fact that he had been blinded and needed to be led by hand.

The bridges at Crevecoeur, which were reported to have been destroyed, were not and were used by the German artillery coming forward in support of their men; this was not done without significant losses however, as the bridges came under British machine-gun fire.

87 Brigade in Marcoing, a mile to the left, came under gas and heavy explosive bombardment from the early hours of the 30th. These destroyed all their telephone communications, not that those to Divisional HQ would have been of any value, given the dire straits to which that had been reduced. Gee's runner did arrive safely, so that Brigadier-General Lucas was able to take measures to safeguard his

The workhorse of the British army was the Vickers machine gun which remained in service until the early 1960s. Water is being added to the cooling jacket.

right flank. 1/KOSB were sent to Marcoing Copse, which was narrow and several hundred yards long, to the south east of the village and south of the canal. Before they reached the copse, however, they came upon the enemy who had already come up from the direction of Les Rues Vertes. The KOSB advanced steadily and drove the Germans back through the wood; until all who were left were either dead, wounded or had been made prisoner (of whom there were fifty).

De Lisle had now established himself in a new Headquarters in Villers Plouich. He read the situation correctly; a staff officer was sent to Brigadier-General Nelson, commanding the reserve 88 Brigade, and ordered him to move up and form the Division's defensive right flank.

The KOSB took up position to the south of the wood, whilst the four battalions of 88 Brigade, which had also become involved in the tussle around the copse, took up position to the left of the KOSB - from left of the KOSB to the canal were 2/Hants, 4/Worcesters, 1/Essex and the Newfoundlanders. The KOSB, divorced from its own brigade, came under Nelson's command. Men of 2/SWB were sent back across the canal by Brigadier-General Lucas to clear up any pockets of German resistance, and then took up a position to connect the Newfoundland Battalion with the R Guernsey LI of 86 Brigade, now on the left of Les Rues Vertes. The KOSB linked with 7/KOYLI of 20th Division near the

Hindenburg Support system, and a new line was then dug.

Despite the quite traumatic day, 'our' three divisions of III Corps had established a right flank from Masnieres to La Vacquerie. Their actions that day had prevented what might well have been an utter disaster.

Rupprecht's men had not achieved what had been planned, though it had been far from being a bad day. Villers Guislain had been taken, but only after they had been seriously – fatally, perhaps – delayed by Vincent's Force. Metz en Couture was now out of the question. His losses had been heavy. But it had been an exercise whose significance would not be lost. German failure had lain in the fact that when the attackers had been reduced to small groups of troops by the continuing battle they failed to operate successfully, losing cohesion, direction and purpose. This operation was a form of fore-runner for the great Spring Offensive of 1918; and the suitable training of the infantry to deal with this sort of situation was a vital part of the preparation for that attack.

December 1st - December 7th 1917. The Last Days of the Battle

The British determined on a counter attack with the intention of taking Villers Guislain and the line of posts two thousand yards to the east of Vaucellette Farm, which ran down for almost three miles, to the north of Lempire – ie much of the ground lost by the 55th Division. East of Gouzeaucourt the attack aimed to recapture Gauche Wood and then Gonnelieu. The Cavalry Corps was involved, mainly the 5th Cavalry Division. These men would, more often than not, be required to operate in the dismounted role – something for which they had for many years been trained.

The attack to the south, near Vaucellette Farm was not a great success, and casualties were heavy, both amongst horses and men. To the north the Guards Division and the dismounted 18/Lancers recaptured Gauche Wood in an attack that began at 6.30 am.

6/Ox and Bucks, with two companies of 5/Northants, were still astride the stretch of main road from Gouzeaucourt to Gonnelieu and in Green Switch trench, between the road and the latter village. 4/Grenadiers passed through them with the objective of retaking Gonnelieu; however the attack was launched just as the Germans were about to start their own. Gonnelieu was therefore full of Germans from the 14th Bavarian Reserve Regiment and the 4th Assault Battalion. The Grenadiers, supported by 1/W Guards on their right, made for the village; they were not successful, however they did halt German plans for a renewed assault towards La Vacquerie. The Grenadiers suffered

205 casualties (amongst them Viscount Gort, who would command the BEF in 1940) and the Welsh Guards 279; Captain GHT Paton, commanding the Grenadier's Support Company, displayed such courage that he was posthumously awarded the Victoria Cross.

The Germans began their attack with a violent bombardment before the infantry set off, at 8.30 am. At La Vacquerie the Germans advanced from Gonnelieu and towards the positions held by 12/RB and 12/KRRC of 60 Brigade. The attack on these two weak and tired battalions was very heavy and by mid-morning parties of the 109th Grenadiers had crossed the main road and were into the outer defences of the village, Village Lane and Barrier Trench. The battalions withdrew inwards, forming a U shaped front, and denied the German's further entrance as they advanced through Sonnet Farm. The arrival of 1/Grenadiers enabled

Captain GHT Paton

the force to push the Germans back over the main road. Halfway through the day 12/RB, separated from its own division for so long, dead beat and sadly depleted, was withdrawn. 12/KRRC, who had defended Sonnet Farm so bravely, were in a similar dire situation; in

La Vacquerie, en route to complete destruction.

Captain Paton leading the counter-attack which won him the VC posthumously.

the afternoon they retook Village Lane and Vacant Alley, two trenches on the La Vacquerie side of the main road, but only after some fierce hand to hand fighting. They were withdrawn at nightfall.

The 61st (South Midland) Division was brought up to relieve the 12th and 20th Divisions, which had been in the battle for twelve days. 2/5 Warwicks relieved 12/KRRC; and during the night of the 1st/2nd December the rest of 183 Brigade relieved the survivors of the 12th Division and what was left of 59 and 60 Brigades of the 20th Division. This only left 61 Brigade in the line from the 20th Division; it was holding the top end of Welsh Ridge, just below and behind the 29th Division. It was relieved, in due course, by 182 Brigade.

The 12th (Eastern) Division had suffered 4,906 casualties, the greatest of any of the divisions that fought at Cambrai; the 20th (Light) had 2,816 of whom some 1,300 were missing – of these perhaps half had been taken prisoner.

Brigadier-General Cheape's 86 Brigade were attacked in their Les Rues Vertes position at 8.15 am, the R Guernsey LI being the first to come under severe attack. From a machine-gun position built in the Sugar Factory on the far side of the canal they were able to pour fire into the side of the attackers, who were advancing over open ground on the southern side. Heavy casualties were inflicted; and the attack was halted. A further attempt was made to remove 16/Middlesex at Mon Plaisir Farm, but the attack was not in great force and it was repelled. Brigadier-General Lucas had taken over command over the Division and tried to get reinforcements; but in vain. In the middle of the afternoon he told the two other brigade commanders to make their own decisions in the light of events. If Masnieres could not be held (as

Byng wished) then they must withdraw and try to hold the flanks across the canal in front of Marcoing. Whilst this conference was taking place the Germans launched another attack under the cover of the heaviest bombardment that the Division had thus far experienced. It reduced both Masnieres and Les Rues Vertes to smoking ruins. Three battalions were engaged on both sides of the canal. The Germans were again ejected from Les Rues Vertes in a fierce close-quarter struggle. They left behind eighty prisoners – Captain Innes, the Brigade Major, and his orderly killed four Germans and captured five others. At 7 pm the Germans gave up their attack on the Brigade.

During the night, after searching for all their wounded and outpost men and joining up with those on the south side of the canal, the whole Brigade withdrew over the northern bank, behind Masnieres. Before dawn on 2 December the Brigade was out of the fight and marching westwards over the Couillet Valley ridge to Ribecourt.

This left 87 and 88 Brigade to hold the reduced front at Marcoing. 87 Brigade, north of the canal, swung its right flank back to the lock bridge by the railway, a thousand yards west of Masnieres. Its left flank was on the railway embankment, near the Cambrai road. The Brigade stood on the east front of the village, holding a front of about a thousand yards.

During the night 88 Brigade swung its left flank back to meet the 87th's at the canal, whilst its right flank rested a thousand yards south of the Masnieres's – Marcoing track. These moves were completed before dawn.

At 8.30 am the Germans began attacking again at the canal bend on its northern bank, but 2/SWB easily stopped them. Although the Welshmen spent the rest of their day under mortar fire, they were spared further assaults.

In fact Crown Prince Rupprecht had decided that 2 December would be a day of respite and reorganisation for his own, very tired, men. Byng had decided to reinforce Marcoing and by daybreak on 3 December 16 Brigade (6th Division) arrived at its south western end.

On 3 December Rupprecht had another go at capturing the canal and shelled Marcoing and the British positions to the west so heavily that the battered troops of 86 Brigade, settling down to enjoy a rest at Ribecourt, were moved a further two miles to the west, over the Trescault Ridge.

To the north of 87 Brigade's left flank 71 Brigade (also of 6th Division) arrived; they were attacked by Germans trying to cut through between Noyelles and Marcoing. 14/DLI fought a ferocious battle

CAMBRAI 1917

30 NOVEMBER

GERMAN ATTACKS ON VII AND III CORPS

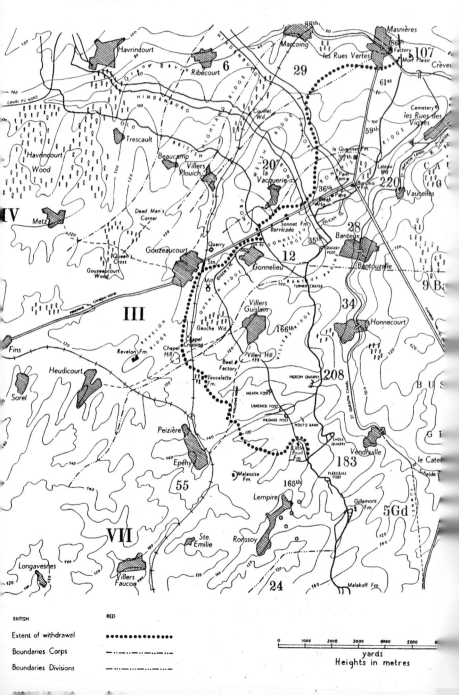

BRITISH	RED
Extent of withdrawal	••••••••••••
Boundaries Corps	—··—··—··—
Boundaries Divisions	—·—·—·—

yards
Heights in metres

here, losing before nightfall 276 officers and men out of a battalion strength of only 450. Captain AM Lascelles won a VC after a truly heroic performance. His citation reads:

After a very heavy bombardment during which Captain Lascelles was wounded, the enemy attacked in strong force but was driven off, success being due in a great degree to the fine example set by this officer, who, refusing to allow his wound to be dressed, continued to encourage his men and organise the defence. Shortly afterwards the enemy again attacked and captured the trench, taking several of his men prisoners. Captain Lascelles at once jumped onto the parapet and followed by the remainder of his company, twelve men only, rushed across under very heavy machine-gun fire and drove over sixty of the enemy back, thereby saving a most critical situation. He was untiring in reorganising the position, but shortly afterwards the enemy again attacked and captured the trench, and Captain Lascelles, who later escaped. The remarkable determination and gallantry of this officer in the course of operations, during which he received two further wounds, afforded an inspiring example to all.

Captain AM Lascelles

Lascelles had fought in the Boer War, won an MC on the Somme (where he had also been wounded) and went back to the Western Front, despite the fact that his right arm was useless, after the events at Cambrai. He was killed on 7 November 1918, the last battle in which the battalion to which he was attached, 15/DLI, fought. He is buried at Dourlers Communal Cemetery Extension, about fifteen miles south of Maubeuge (II. C.24).

With the arrival of 16 and 18 Brigades of the 6th Division, arrangements were made to withdraw the left flank of the 29th Division, and some of 87 Brigade came out of the line. Two battalions of the 87th, 2/SWB and the Newfoundlanders, reinforced 88 Brigade. Both of these units had taken very heavy casualties on 3 December from the furious German bombardment and their subsequent probing infantry attacks.

During the night of the 3rd it was decided that it was no longer tenable to hold a line north of the canal, and all the troops were brought back. In the dark of the morning of 4 December 455 Field Company RE blew the remaining five main bridges. 88 Brigade was still at the front but now stood, facing east, on a line running from below Marcoing with its right to the north of Welsh Ridge. Relief finally came on the 5th, when 108 Brigade of the 36th (Ulster) Division took their place. The Division had suffered 4,232 casualties, not far short of those inflicted upon the 12th Division. 88 Brigade had been constantly in battle for fifteen days.

One battalion was to get a singular honour. In recognition of its achievements at Gallipoli, the Somme (Beaumont Hamel especially recalled today in the Memorial Park), Arras and Third Ypres as well as at Cambrai; the Newfoundland Regiment was accorded the title Royal. It was the only unit to have this honour bestowed upon it during the Great War; indeed only two other battalions had ever had such an honour bestowed on them whilst hostilities were in progress – the 18th of Foot in 1695 and the Royal Berkshire Regiment in 1885.

Haig and Byng decided that they should withdraw their men to a defensible line for the winter – and in the light of an expected all-out assault by the Germans in the Spring of 1918. On the night of 4 December the withdrawal commenced, and was completed by dawn on the 7th. The salient had been reduced to an average depth of two and a half miles over a length of six miles; the Germans had made gains

Gouzeaucourt under German occupation 1916.

Ground recaptured, standing before their trophy and unconcerned by the body of a British soldier, these Germans pose for a photographic record of their triumph.

almost equalling that to the south of the Gouzeaucourt road.

Rupprecht made two further attacks in this area, in the hope of gaining rather better positions. One was at La Vacquerie, between 2 and 6 December. Here a sixth Victoria Cross was won – all within a mile radius of this utterly forgettable hamlet. 9/RInnF (Royal Inniskilling Fusiliers) was in support of 2/7 Warwicks on 6 December, preparing to hand over the line to the 63rd (Royal Naval) Division, at the north end of Welsh Ridge, in Ostrich Trench. Second Lieutenant JS Emerson of the Fusiliers was awarded a posthumous VC for his action in fighting off German bombers, despite his wounds. His body, like that of Captain Wain VC, killed nearby, was never recovered. His memorial is a name at

Second Lieutenant JS Emerson

Louverval; and who knows but the remains of these two gallant men may still be in the fields around La Vacquerie.

The attack against the Royal Naval Division on Welsh Ridge could, if it had been successful, have had very dangerous consequences to the remaining British salient; though the Germans later reported that it was only a matter of gaining an improved defensive position. The battle took place in driving snow on the 30th and 31st December; it cost the Division 1,434 casualties; whilst the Germans used fourteen battalions, either in the assault or to hold their line.

It was appropriate, perhaps, that the last stirrings of the uproar created by the British attack on 20 November should come to an end on New Year's Eve.

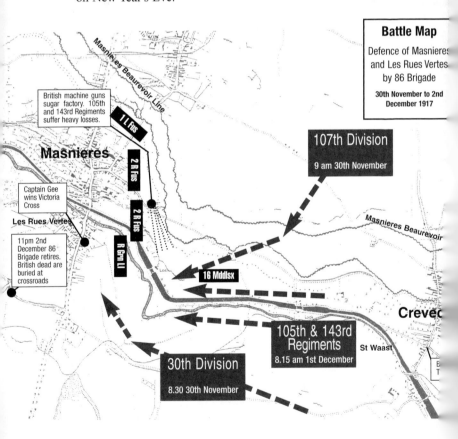

Battle Map

Defence of Masnieres and Les Rues Vertes by 86 Brigade

30th November to 2nd December 1917

British machine guns sugar factory. 105th and 143rd Regiments suffer heavy losses.

1 L Fus

2 R Fus

2 R Fus

R Gen LI

Masnieres

Captain Gee wins Victoria Cross

Les Rues Vertes

11pm 2nd December 86 Brigade retires. British dead are buried at crossroads

107th Division

9 am 30th November

Masnieres Beaurevoir

16 Mddlsx

Crevec

105th & 143rd Regiments

8.15 am 1st December

St Waast

30th Division

8.30 30th November

Chapter Five

THE NEW ZEALAND ASSAULT:
29 SEPTEMBER – 5 OCTOBER 1918

The New Zealand Division (1918)
Major General Sir AH Russell KCB KCMG
Order of Battle

1st NZ Brigade	2nd NZ Brigade	3rd NZ Brigade
(*Brigade-General CW Melville*)	(*Brigadier-General R Young*)	(*Brigadier-General H Hart*)
1/ Auckland Regiment	1/Canterbury Regiment	1/Rifle Brigade
2/Auckland Regiment	2/Canterbury Regiment	2/Rifle Brigade
1/Wellington Regiment	I/Otago Regiment	3/Rifle Brigade
2/Wellington Regiment	2/Otago Regiment	4/Rifle Brigade

New Zealand Pioneer Battalion (Maori)
1, 2, 3 NZ Field Ambulance

The situation of the German army by the late summer of 1918 was bleak. The great series of offensives in the spring and early summer of 1918, whilst showing great promise, had come to naught. Indeed, they had so weakened the ability of the German army to sustain counter blows that they certainly were the main contributory factor to Germany's defeat in the late autumn of 1918.

On the other hand, there were possibilities for Germany as the summer of 1918 drew on; if she could hold out for another year, if she could make the price of victory too great, it was still possible that peace terms might be reached which could be acceptable to the German political nation and the military machine. There were two factors that could spoil this scenario, one of which was the unravelling and defeat of Germany's allies. Whilst not necessarily an immediate threat, obviously total collapse of her allied Central European and Turkish powers would pose a serious problem. The other was a concerted effort by the Western allies to set about ending the war by military means. This seemed unlikely, given the battering inflicted in

Sir Douglas Haig reviewing the New Zealand Division. It was amongst the finest of the British and Dominion divisions that saw service in the Great War. TAYLOR LIBRARY

Commanding Officer: Major General AH Russell

the spring, particularly on the British, who at this stage of the war posed the principal military threat to Germany. To make as certain as possible that this eventually did not come about, Ludendorff placed a disproportionate force opposite the British lines – both in quantity and quality; and also set about systematically restoring the Hindenburg Line defences, now many miles behind the front line. This war could be made to run.

The events of 8 August, and the subsequent assaults, proved to be a blow to Germany's hopes; but the Hindenburg Line still offered a possible hope of containing the tide of the allied advance. In fact it was not to be.

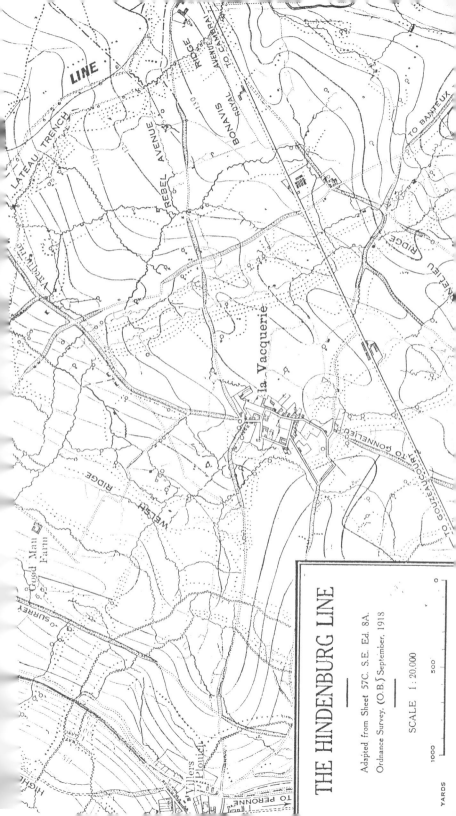

THE HINDENBURG LINE

Adapted from Sheet 57C. S.E. Ed. 8A.
Ordnance Survey, (O.B.) September, 1918

SCALE 1:20,000

YARDS   1000   500   0

The New Zealand Pioneer Battalion constructing a new plank road.
TAYLOR LIBRARY

Coming before the section of the Hindenburg Line, covered in detail earlier in this book, on 28 August 1918 was the New Zealand Division, taking over the thrust forward from the 42nd (East Lancs) Division. The New Zealand Division had an awesome reputation on the Western Front – well led, well officered, well motivated and with a high quality of fighting men. If not the finest, it was certainly amongst the finest of the British and Dominion divisions that saw service in the Great War; a brilliance that is, for some strange reason, rather unknown.

At midday on 28 September Major-General Russell, whose

Headquarters were in Velu Wood, five miles west of Trescault, came forward to hold a conference at his 1 Brigade HQ in Neuville Bourjonval. His orders were to carry Welsh Ridge and La Vacquerie; then cross the Bonavis Ridge and seize the crossings of the St Quentin Canal and River Escaut between Vaucelles on the right and Crevecoeur, two and half miles downstream. This was to be an advance of four miles on a two mile front.

Immediately in front of the Division was a long steep hill; there had been no time for reconnaissance. Two thousand yards up the slope was La Vacquerie, once more a strongly defended part of the Hindenburg Line, and from which all the ground between it and the Couillet Valley could be observed. The Division's maps were out of date. The attack would be in the dark and therefore dependent on compass bearings. They would have to cross numerous and confusing old trench systems – mainly British, from fighting in 1917 and early 1918 – with all that entailed – gaping holes, remnants of wire, cable over which to trip and all the detritus of a contemporary battlefield. The German artillery remained both powerful and competent, and already was bombarding the approaches to the Line. The positive features for the night's operations were the fact that it was dry, the moon was waning and there was a slight mist. The Division would assault with two brigades up, the 1st on the left, the 2nd on the right and the 3rd in reserve. Zero hour was to be 3.30 am, Sunday 29 September.

The brigades assembled north east of Villers Plouich at the bottom of Couillet Valley between the railway and Surrey Road Trench four hundred yards away up the slope. At 3 am the Lancastrians of the 42 Division, occupying positions slightly forward, were withdrawn and the New Zealand artillery barrage commenced; the German reply was not slow in coming, though falling mainly behind the assembled infantry.

Two companies of 1/Canterbury of 2 Brigade went forward on time and by dawn, after a lengthy struggle in the ruins, had overcome the defenders of La Vacquerie. The supporting companies should have come up by then, but had got hopelessly bewildered by the labyrinth of trenches and the confusion of wire. They deviated to the right, out of the Division's sector, and set off towards the Gouzeaucourt to Cambrai road. This was something of a disaster, as the neighbouring 5th Division had faced its own significant problems in its attack. One of the companies became engaged in heavy fighting and sixty of the men were surrounded and captured at about 10.30 am. An officer and one of the men, wounded, were put in a dugout for protection and were

Men of the Auckland Regiment moving up to the line.   TAYLOR LIBRARY

liberated in the subsequent advance. The other company became involved in equally heavy fighting, but was able to withdraw to the 5th Division's lines. North of the village, where the German line had always been deep, the Aucklands and Wellingtons met strong resistance but had overcome it by 6 am and taken 250 prisoners. 2 Brigade brought forward the Otago battalions as the morning progressed to assist in overcoming the remaining stubborn defences about La Vacquerie. By mid-afternoon the Canterburys had finally dealt with all the village defence complex and had moved over the main road to Bleak House from where they could look at Lateau Wood. For now they had to reorganise and consolidate; the German defences around Bonavis damaged, but resolute.

2 Brigade had failed to take all its objectives, but had done well. It had suffered numerous casualties, but had taken the formidable obstacle of La Vacquerie, which acted as something of a gateway to the canal approach, had taken a thousand prisoners and severely dislocated the German defences.

1 Brigade, with the Wellingtons on the right and Aucklands on the left, had swept all before them in the remaining hours of darkness. Before daylight they had crossed Welsh Ridge and gone into the La Vasquerie Valley, overwhelming resistance and capturing hundreds of

prisoners. By 6 am the battalions had arrived at the main road between the Bonavis junction and Masnieres, touching the northern edge of Lateau Wood near to Le Quennet Farm. Their casualties had been very light, not more than a hundred for both battalions. Because of the confusing condition of the battlefield, two platoons of 2/Auckland had gone astray in the dark and moved right across to the other flank of the Brigade. They found themselves on the right of the Wellingtons and in the ruins of Bonavis Farm, which they held until the Otagos came up to help them.

1 Brigade was well on its way to achieving the time scale set. 1/Auckland pushed ahead over the road, heading for Crevecoeur, and at 8 am captured two heavy guns and their crews. However the Brigade had become too widely stretched in the darkness; to the dismay of its commander, Lieutenant-Colonel SS Allen, 2/Auckland and its sister battalion were obliged to withdraw to the main road. The Brigade, with the Wellingtons on the right at Bonavis Ridge, was now consolidated in anticipation of an advance on the canal. By noon the Division had taken some 1,400 prisoners, two naval guns, thirty field guns and 200 machine-guns. This latter figure was particularly significant for the long term; despite enourmous quantities of automatic firepower, the Germans were unable to hold their positions. One of the greatest strengths of the German army lay in the quality of its machine-gun crews. So many of these had been lost in the preceding months that this vital stiffener to German defensive capability had been largely lost.

Both brigades now looked over a sight new to them on the Western Front. It was a country largely untouched by war – certainly in contrast to that which they had just crossed. The assaults and defences here in November and December 1917 had casued relatively little damage to the fields and woods. To the left they could see the tall buildings of Cambrai wreathed in smoke, a consequence of British shelling and, more significantly, the German withdrawal, accompanied as it was by the blowing up of stores and ammunition dumps and the setting on fire of the town.

1 Brigade was instructed to move forward about 2,500 yards down the slope to the canal and Les Rues des Vignes. 2 Brigades's efforts would be directed towards Vaucelles, on the far bank of the St Quentin canal and the River Escaut, at the foot of some steeply rising ground, backed by Cheneaux Wood, a large and undamaged mass of trees. It would be the task of the Otagos to take the bridge crossing the waterway, a couple of thousand yards in front of them.

The rest of the day was spent in regrouping – one of the first requirements, for example, was the bringing forward of artillery support and replenishing rations and ammunition. This section of the canal and river had never been crossed before, defying all Byng's efforts ten months earlier. During the day the far bank was carefully scrutinised, which made it quite clear that the far bank was very strongly held. A further complication came with a turn in the weather, raining heavily and turning the ground soft and muddy.

The attack was to commence at 5.45 am on 30 September; but as night fell 2/Otago sent patrols down to the western side of the canal to examine the defences. The Germans were found to be in position in strength, so no attempt was made to pre-empt the early morning attack. However, the Germans realised that the New Zealanders were about to strike and withdrew over both waterways into Vaucelles. 2/Otago therefore left their probing patrols in position at the bottom of the slope and reinforced them.

It rained heavily all night but the sky cleared at about 4 am. Soon afterwards Lieutenant RD Douglas led a patrol, under severe rifle and machine-gun fire from the village, to the iron and wooden lock bridges that crossed the canal two hundred yards west of the village. He found that the iron span had been blown, whilst from their commanding heights the German machine-guns could sweep the ground west of the bridge, preventing any attempt to cross. Lieutenant TK Broadgate, of the Engineers, and a small party went forward to see what could be done to make the bridge passable, but he was killed and his men driven off.

Another patrol, led by an intrepid sergeant of 2/Otago, R Fitzgerald, explored about a mile and a half further south from the broken bridge, looking for alternative crossing points. North of Banteux, where the canal narrows, he found that the down stream lock bridge had been mined. He removed the fuzes from the explosives, despite being in full view of the Germans. He carried on further up stream, surprised at the seeming total lack of Germans, and came to the main road bridge at the southern end of the village. Here he came upon four German sappers who were preparing to destroy the bridge. The patrol killed one of them and forced the others to beat a hasty retreat across the bridge. The patrol went after them, all unaware of what they might come across and entered Bantouzelle. They moved through it to the eastern edge without seeing any of the enemy.

At this stage Fitzgerald decided that the better part of wisdom was to return with his valuable information to battalion HQ; the CO put patrols close to the waterway on the western bank.

All had not been entirely peaceful on the ridge above. Pockets of German resistance remained in parts of the Hindenbug Line to the east of La Vacquerie, and it took 1/Canterbury until the evening to clear these after much close-quarter fighting.

Sergeant Fitzgerald's patrol had been lucky – all the Germans had by no means left either Banteux or Bantouzelle. With their position secured on the right by the 5th Division, which had made good its objectives during the day, 1/Canterbury set off at 5.45 am on their planned advance from their positions south of the Gouzeaucourt road and the Bonavis junction, overcoming desultory resistance. By 8 am they arrived at the Sugar Factory on the north edge of Banteux to find that all the garrison had fled across the canal, the partly destroyed bridge there being passable in single file. With no sign of the enemy, two platoons of the Canterburys went over the bridge and took up

New Zealanders take advantage of the shelter offered by a sunken road.
TAYLOR LIBRARY

position among the willow trees which lined the canal for most of its route through the valley. To the left the rest of the Brigade had moved up in support to a position a thousand yards west of the canal, hoping to take the waterway between Banteux and Vaucelles. Meanwhile the Germans had returned in force to the eastern side of the canal and forced the Canterburys back over the bridge; posts were established to watch and to wait.

2 Brigade now stayed, watched and waited. They needed the 5th Division to come up on the right (they had been held up by stubborn resistance further south). 2 Brigade's guard of the right flank of the Division continued until 5 October.

1 Brigade's assault got off to a bad start. The runners with the orders for that morning for the two lead battalion, 1/Wellington and 2/Auckland, lined up over the main road to Masnieres, got lost in the dark and did not reach the battalion Headquarters until almost midnight. The CO of 1/Wellington, Lieutenant-Colonel FK Turnbull DSO MC, misunderstood his orders, and did not attack as planned. He thought he should move at 5 am and when the artillery barrage did not take place he assumed that the attack was cancelled. 2/Auckland, on the other hand, went forward on time, heading for the bridges at Crevecoeur. When Turnbull became aware of what was going on he took his men forward, setting off at about 6 am. Despite fierce oppostion from artillery and machine-gun fire on the far side of the canal, by 8 am he had occupied Les Rues des Vignes, the southern end of which had already been cleared by 2/Auckland. However the devastating bombardment of the village, which continued during the day and causing the battalion many casualties, meant that it could not be consolidated until after dark. A search for a crossing point showed that both bridges had been destroyed.

All had not been plain sailing for Lieutenant-Colonel Allen, either. The runners to his own companies in 2/Auckland got lost in the dark and the maze of trenches; he had to change his plans. Captain J Evans was sent with his company to seize the crossings of both the canal and the river at Crevecoeur; once these were secured, two more companies would continue the advance through the village. However his lack of knowledge of the waterways at Crevecoeur and its fateful stone bridge, together with the resolve of the Germans to defend this essential access point not only to the Masnieres-Beaurevoir Line but to the villages leading to the strategically vital town of Caudry, made these orders impossible to fulfill.

The entrance to Crevecoeur is guarded by both waterways. The canal comes straight up from Les Rues des Vignes and then makes a sharp left turn south of the village. The Escaut, usually running parallel to the canal, makes a sharp turn to the left at almost the same point. The result was to produce a large, four hundred yards wide by three hundred yards, long marsh – effectively an island. The stone bridge, the entrance to Crevecoeur, lies over the river at the far side of the marsh. The canal's two span, badly damaged, narrow iron bridge was impassable. The canal could be crossed by way of a half destroyed wooden foot bridge further down stream, almost opposite the stone bridge.

Regardless of the confusion, Captain Evans did do very well. Within forty five minutes of setting off he had taken his company (the 15th) a mile and a half across open country. By 6.30 am one of his platoons was on the footbridge and moving cautiously towards the stone crossing of the river. His other platoons had meanwhile got onto the western half of the island, but were without any cover. As his platoon got closer to the stone bridge they saw that it had been mined, with wires running below the stonework of the crossing. They could do nothing about this, because the Germans spotted them and poured a stream of machine-gun fire across the bridge, killing the platoon commander, his sergeant and a number of other men. Corporal A Steward survived the blast of fire and took cover in a ditch, secure from

Bridge over the River Selle at Briastre which was reconstructed by New Zealand engineers in thirteen hours under intense shell fire. Troops crossing the bridge are moving north east towards 'Belleview' and Bedudienies. <small>TAYLOR LIBRARY</small>

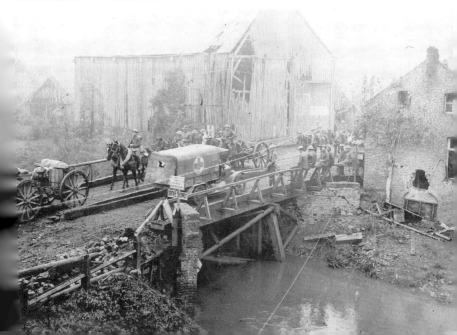

machine-gun fire but cut off from his Company Commander by a narrow branch of the river, which divided the marsh.

One of his men, Private James Crichton, although wounded in the foot, volunteered to take a message to Captain Evans to tell him of the situation. He lowered himself into the narrow branch of the river and swam across under a hail of fire directed at no-one but him; he then ran across the open ground to join his captain, reporting the mines but neglecting to mention his wounded foot.

In answer to his question as to whether the mines could be removed after dark, Crichton told Evans that he thought it possible. He then made his way back to Steward, who was still vainly trying to gather together all his men. Crichton crawled forward towards the stone bridge, still under machine-gun fire, in search of his lost comrades. On arrival at the bridge he decided to have an attempt at safeguarding the bridge there and then. Hidden from view by the masonry of the bridge, he swam underneath it and removed both detonators and mines, throwing the explosive charges into the water, but retaining the detonators. He once more made the perilous journey back to Evans, told him the bridge was safe and showed him the detonators.

Private James Crichton

Evans would not let the bitterly cold – soaked several times – and wounded man return to Steward and his trapped force. He was sent back over the river as a stretcher bearer for a severely wounded soldier. At the Aid Post his foot was examined and dressed and the Padre then ordered him back to battalion HQ. Crichton was awarded the Victoria Cross, survived the war (ending it as a sergeant) and died in Auckland in 1961.

Steward was forced to remain in his vulnerable position all day – there was no way in which he could get his party back safely under both the unceasing fire and attempts by the Germans to encircle him. When darkness fell he was surrounded and then taken prisoner, along with eleven of his men, although others managed to evade the enemy and made it back to Captain Evans' position.

Here the three platoons still held their ground, despite heavy bombardment. Colonel Allen sent two more platoons over to join them whilst the rest of the battalion came up to the western bank of the canal, but made not further attempt to cross over. 2/Auckland stayed there until 1 October, the following day, when Crevecoeur was

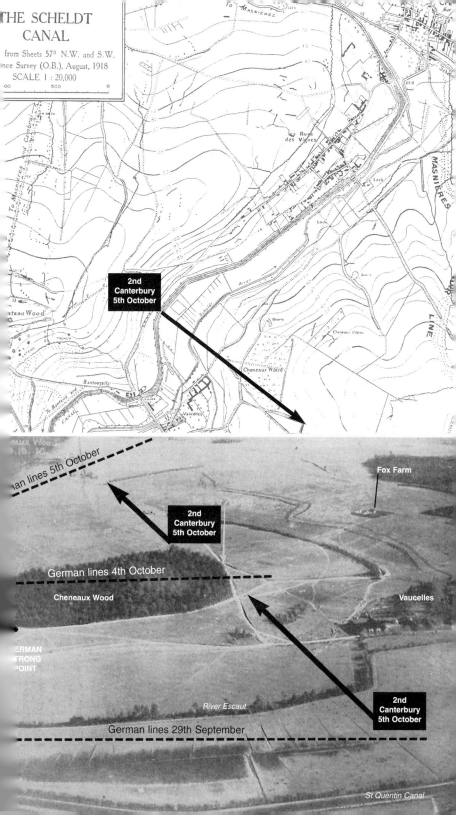

THE SCHELDT CANAL

from Sheets 57ᴮ N.W. and S.W.
nce Survey (O.B.), August, 1918
SCALE 1 : 20,000

2nd Canterbury 5th October

German lines 5th October

2nd Canterbury 5th October

Fox Farm

German lines 4th October

Cheneaux Wood

Vaucelles

GERMAN STRONG POINT

2nd Canterbury 5th October

River Escaut

German lines 29th September

St Quentin Canal

captured – but not by way of the stone bridge. The Battalion had taken heavy casualties by that stage – eleven officers and 143 other ranks killed or wounded (including the Second in Command, Major E Sherson) and the eleven men captured from Corporal Steward's platoon. Corps Headquarters did not have a clear idea of the sitiuation. It was wrongly understood that the 62nd Division, on the northern side of the canal, had advanced on Seranvillers, two miles to the north east of Crevecoeur; and that troops could be put through Crevecoeur in large numbers and that the bridge was secured. Accordingly a squadron of 3/Hussars was attached to 1 Brigade with orders to cross the canal and make contact with the 62nd Division at Seranvillers. 1/Auckland was to pass through 2/Auckland in support of the cavalry.

When the Hussars arrived at the Battalion HQ behind Les Rues des Vignes they not only saw their commander killed by shell fire, but also saw that there was no chance of crossing that evening, or even the following day, 1 October, unless there was a dramatic change in the situation. They withdrew. Russell revised his plans for 1 October. He would move his 1 Brigade over the canal to the north, thereby by-passing Crevecoeur to the north, and would cross by way of the intact wooden bridge which led to Mon Plaisir Farm.

2/Wellington would sweep around, keeping close to the canal, and then attack the village along the road leading westwards towards Masnieres. 1/Auckland was to move on the left flank and were to keep in touch with the 3rd Division, which had replaced the 62nd.

The objective was a formidable one, especially for 1/Auckland. It lay two thousand yards ahead of the start line, on higher ground and through the Masnieres-Beaurevoir Line, which formed a redoubt about the village; this particular part of the line came to an end at a track leading northwards at the western end of Lesdain, itself well garrisoned.

On the night of the 30th, under the cover of darkness and rain, the two battalions moved down to the canal,

crossed it and before dawn were in position, facing east on a narrow frontage of seven hundred yards. The artillery barrage was set for 6 am.

As the infantry set off under the covering fire they came under sustained German bombardment and shell fire from the higher ground behind the village. By 8 am, despite strong resistance, 2/Wellington had advanced to the church in the centre of the village, having taken 150 prisoners. Their own casualties were heavy, largely caused by the enfilade fire coming from the artillery and machine-guns on the higher ground.

Second Lieutenant H Petit was advancing through the village between the main road, going east, and a short parallel street two hundred yards to the left, when he bumped into a group of Germans withdrawing to their defence line between the two villages. He pursued them and took prisoner thirty of them, though they were not to know that they were being threatened by an empty revolver. The Battalion had, however, reached the limit of its advance and had suffered over 150 casualties.

The stone bridge was at long last cleared; 2/Auckland crossed it and

New Zealand troops observing a barrage on German positions.

the two battalions established a strong defence perimeter around its eastern end during the course of the rest of the morning. The northward bearing track, Mill Road, was where the Wellingtons stopped; part of the Masnieres-Beaurevoir Line and well defended, it was to cause 1/Auckland severe problems when they attacked at 6 am.

1/Auckland had to cope with a long slope coming down on their left flank, crossed by a series of four tracks or roads, all part of the Masnieres-Beaurevoir Line. This was a part of the line that had been strengthened by the Germans in recent months. The first of these ran from Crevecoeur to Rumilly; the second was a sunken road going north to Cambrai, and was marked by a Calvary about a thousand yards beyond the jumping off point; the third was narrow and sunken in parts, about five hundreds yard further on; and the fourth was Mill Road, just in front of the perimeter established by 2/Wellington and 2/Auckland.

1/Auckland set off on time and two companies made short work of the Germans on the Rumilly road; the position was taken within the hour. The second objective was defended by a considerable amount of barbed wire and the enemy was well dug-in, making full use of the sunken road. By 8 am the opposition here had been overcome, despite the fact that the front of the two company advance was covered by forty machine-guns and two hundred men surrendered to them. As they set off for the third road the battalion came under heavy fire from the left, Seranvillers defences (which had not yet fallen to the advancing 3rd Division), and from Mill Road. Alderman sent his third company forward, and this supplementary force enabled the two depleted leading companies to take the third road, whilst the Support Company went on to clear Mill Road.

Although the objective had been achieved the left flank of 1/Auckland was very exposed to the left – more so than before. As the morning progressed the Germans launched a very heavy counter attack, endeavouring to recapture the Old Mill Road line. Under a storm of shellfire that fell on the Division's positions on both sides of the canal, the Germans inched forward on the left so that 1/Auckland had to move westwards to avoid being cut off. The withdrawal was costly, but by 10.30 am the survivors had found shelter in the sunken Crucifix road, the embankments providing a defence line from which to repel the enemy. The Germans contented themselves with retaking their main defence line at the Old Mill Road, realising that Crevecoeur was lost in any case, and would leave them in a vulnerable salient into the New Zealand line. However, south of the Crucifix road they continued to attack 2/Wellington and poured a torrent of fire into 1/Auckland's position.

At noon the Battalion had become so depleted that a company of 1/Wellington, commanded by Captain JR Cade, crossed the canal to take over from them in the sunken road. 1/Auckland was relieved on 3 October; it had suffered 231 casualties, including the Second in Command killed. The Battalion's Medical Officer, Captain PA Ardagh MC, was awarded the DSO, having been recommended for the Victoria Cross, for his heroic efforts in tending the wounded in a totally inadequate dressing station for thirty-six hours non-stop. The four Auckland companies went into action with 3 or 4 officers and 130 men; they came out, respectively with: 1 and 38; 0 and 29; 2 and 51; and 2 and 39.

Foiled for the moment, the New Zealand Division still needed a clear a way for its progress eastwards. The sappers came forward to prepare pontoon bridges to be used over the various waterways, despite coming under the quite ferocious artillery bombardment, one of the worst ever experienced by the Division. On the evening of 2 October the Brigade artillery was moved up to the canal bank at Crevecoeur and to the low-lying area on the north eastern edge of Les Rues des Vignes. The German bombardment continued unceasingly through 3 October, concentrating its attentions on the approaches to and from Crevecoeur, the canal bridges and Captain Cade's company in Crucifix Road. It was considered that the enemy would counter attack against Crucifix Road, so that on the evening of 3 October Brigadier-General Hart took the Rifle Brigade to relieve the Aucklands and Wellingtons. Higher up stream, at Vaucelles, 2 Brigade had been unable to make any crossings of the canal. On 1 October the 37th Division took over that part of the advance, leaving the Canterbury battalions holding the sector north of Vaucelles. At this part the canal makes a sweeping bend to the east, with the Escaut flowing five hundred yards further to the east. There were no intact bridges either there or at Les Rues des Vignes, and the two available locks, the Tordoir and the Vinchy, had both been blown. Cheneux Wood, on the other side of the canal, was still strongly held and guns there would cause heavy casualties if any attempt were made to cross.

On the morning of 5 October there was a fair amount of shelling on both sides of the canal. Captain LB Hutton, on the right flank of 2/Canterbury and adjacent to the 37th Division, felt that this might indicate a German withdrawal. Taking some of his men and a patrol from the 37th Division he managed to get across the broken bridge at

Vaucelles and went through the village, going fourteen hundred yards beyond it, skirting the bottom of Cheneux Copse and getting to Fox Farm, eight hundred yards to the south of it, without seeing any Germans.

Immediately this information got back to Lieutenant-Colonel Stewart he sent a company of his 2/Canterbury over on an improvised raft, three at a time. The Germans had not abandoned the position entirely, however. A platoon under Second Lieutenant Mitchell came across some of them in a sunken road in front of the northern corner of the copse, entrenched in a machine-gun emplacement in a quarry. The enemy were not going to retire easily, but the position was eventually overrun when most of them were killed and the other fifteen (along with five machine-guns) were taken prisoner.

More of the Canterburys and 37th Division could now be brought over on rafts made up by the sappers. Further up, at Les Rues des Vignes, Rifle Brigade battalions began to cross and thus, on 5 October, the New Zealand battle for the canal and river crossings was over.

Steel bridge built over the Canal Du Nord by New Zealand engineers.
TAYLOR LIBRARY

Chapter Six

THE TOURS

Tour 1: The La Vacquerie Battlefield Area.

*This tour is best either walking or on a cycle. It is passable in a car,
but with some difficulty and dependent on weather. The total distance
is something in the region of four miles; Two and a half hours should
be allowed if by foot, the time variable according to how long is spent
in the cemeteries.*

The village is a mile and a half down the D917 from the Bonavis
cross roads; to the left of this junction is Bonavis Farm and in the fields
on the right is Pam Pam Farm. Before the autoroute, on the left, is
Bleak House, whilst the site of Sonnet Farm is in the circle of roads
created by the autoroute access arrangements. Just before the autoroute
access there is a turning to the right to La Vacquerie, a hamlet which is
more or less contained within the square of a minor road. The place is
dominated by its church, and is now a picture of calm, the rumble of
the heavy traffic on the autoroute and the main road below the only
sounds that disturb rural bliss - unless, of
course, the French airforce are engaging
in low flying operations from their
airfield near Cambrai. It is hard to
imagine the mayhem that took place
around this insignificant spot in late 1917
and the autumn of 1918.

Park your car at the church [1]and
take the time to look around you. The
village was at the very front of the
Hindenburg Line, jutting out like an
arrowhead, surrounded by multiple rows
of barbed wire and deep trenches with
many machine-gun posts. To the east, six
hundred yards away, was the second part
of the line, with trenches connecting the
systems. A light railway once ran from the
village northwards towards Masnieres.

Looking north from the village there is
a deeply sunken track, running through

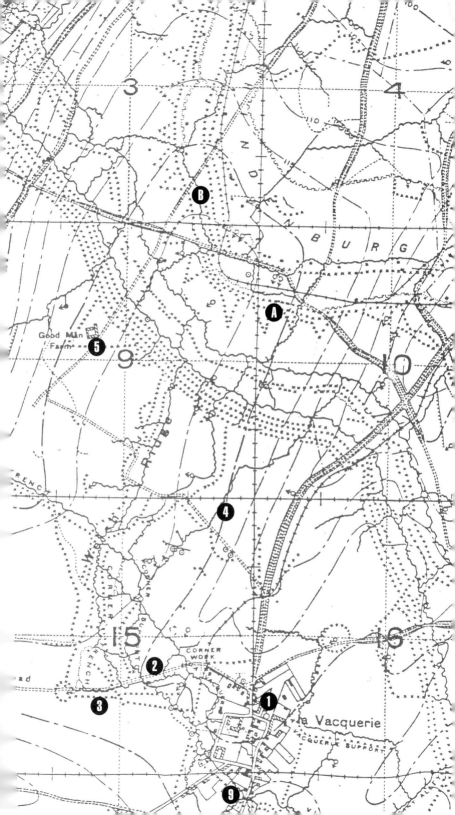

German machine gun bunker at the 'Corner Work'.

Private A E Shepherd

Vacquerie Valley. Walk towards it for a hundred yards or so and at the brick wall of a farm, the last building on the left, turn left up another sunken road. This is Welsh Road, leading to the northern edge of the defence system at the **Corner Work [2]**. About five hundred yards up the lane, close to a wire fence on the left, is a tree growing out of a slab of concrete, once a German machine-gun bunker.

It was here at the Corner Work that 12/KRRC attacked the village on 20 November 1917. It was in the immediate vicinity that Private Shepherd took charge of the situation when all the officers of A Company had become casualties and destroyed the occupants of a machine-gun post, winning himself the Victoria Cross **[3]**. British grenades still lie about here in the grass and ditches and the surface is uneven, the grass hiding the site of the old trench lines and shell holes. Welsh Ridge is over to the right on the rising ground.

It is possible to drive down this narrow track all the way down to Villers Plouich; it crosses the British line at Welsh and Newport Trenches and Surrey Road at the bottom of the slope, traversing No Man's Land as the track descends.

However, this is not part of the route, so return to the road junction

114

and take the left turn, leading into the deeply sunken Vacquerie Valley. After two hundred yards take the track to the left **[4]**.

The ground all around at this point rises gently upward and is devoid of trees. You are now walking between the first and second defences of the Hindenburg Line which ran north westerly from this area, over the high wooded valley side three quarters of a mile ahead. The track takes a sudden turning right.

Stop and look at the relevant battle maps. You are now on top of Welsh Ridge; on the right, down the slope, is **Good Old Man Farm [5]**. The ridge is named after the battles fought by Welsh Regiments in the spring of 1917; some versions have it spelt with a 'c', but here is not the place to discuss the spelling of the Welsh/Welch regiments - the version 'c' was finally adopted after the war.

Also on your right, in the German second line, about three hundred yards beyond the farm, is the site of Ostrich Trench. In due course, when you pass the farm look a hundred yards or so to the right. Somewhere in this area (B) is where Captain Wain won his Victoria Cross; he has no known grave and may well lie under the ground nearby. He was dragged to comparative safety in one of the deep trenches, but his body was lost in subsequent fighting, a common fate for many killed in the war.

Close by, on 6 December 1917, is the site (A) of the action which won Second Lieutenant JS Emerson his Victoria Cross. His battalion, 9/RInnF of the 36th (Ulster) Division, had been brought up to relieve

Looking north on Welsh Ridge towards the scenes of heroism by Second Lieutenants Wain and Emerson.

20th Division attacked towards camera in direction of Vacquerie 20 November 1917

Welsh Ridge

British Front Line, Royal Naval Division, on Welsh Ridge 200 yards west of Germans, 31 December 1917

Germans Front Line, 20 November 1917 and again 3 December 1918

British Line through village 10 am 20 November 1917

British retired to Welsh Ridge 3 December 1917

the 20th Division, exhausted after days in the front edge of this traumatic battle zone.

Your walk thus far will have taken you across three British trenches of 1917, Ostrich, Welsh and Welsh Support. 17 and 19/RWF (Royal Welsh Fusiliers) and 12/SWB (South Wales Borderers) of 119 Brigade, 40th Division paid a high price when they pushed the Germans back behind their Hindenburg Line here at La Vacquerie in April and May 1917; it is no surprise that the ridge had the name Welsh bestowed upon it. During that hard-fought battle the Welshmen actually bombed their way into the village; when the leading bombers ran out of grenades they carried on the fight through the barbed wire with knobkerries and weighted sticks as well as the bayonet - the nature of close-quarter fighting was (is?) primaeval.

On 20 November 1917, at 6.20 am, in its charge for the bridges on the St Quentin canal, the 20th (Light) Division came up this slope after assembling in the valley below, having previously been assembled in the dense Couillet Wood to your immediate north, on the far side of the valley. The Division's three brigades were assembled from La Vacquerie to three quarters of a mile or so to your right, advancing behind some seventy tanks which crushed the dense barbed wire as they came, terrorising the defenders, who were also being shattered by the artillery barrage that seemed to come from nowhere.

Between the church in the hamlet and the area where you are standing came the men of 7/DCLI, 7/SLI, 7/KOYLI and 12/King's (King's Liverpool Regiment). Beyond them, to the north east, were the four battalions of 60 Brigade, accompanied by Captain Wain with his six tanks.

To the south west came 36 Brigade of the 12th (Eastern) Division, straddling the main road, the D917, advancing through the southern half of La Vacquerie. Three hours later the three brigades of the 29th Division set off from their reserve positions in the valley between Gouzeaucourt and Villers Plouich, the latter of which may be seen to the west, in the valley below. Something like seven thousand men and a hundred and fifty tanks came up the hill this morning,

29th Division did not have things all their own way; over to your right, a thousand yards or so away, where the autoroute crosses the Vacquerie Valley, in the direction of Masnieres, is where 1/Essex was held up by the German strong point on the north eastern corner of Welsh Ridge. The obstacle was removed by them with the assistance of four tanks.

The 63rd (Naval) Division defended this ridge against Crown Prince

Good Old Man Farm, taken by 42nd East Lancs Division 28 September 1918 in final battle by New Zealand Division for Welsh Ridge

La Vacquerie

Both front lines after battles 31 December 1917

Welsh Ridge

Surrey Road Long Communication Trench

Start lines for both assaults on La Vacquerie 20 November 1917 and 28 September 1918 at this road

Villers Plouich ➞

View from the road in the bottom of Couillet Valley looking up the forward slope and battlefield of Wesh Ridge.

Rupprecht's final counter stroke in the last days of December 1917. Very close to this spot, in January 1918, a truce took place in No Man's Land. A large number of Germans left their front line trench and beckoned to members of the RND (Royal Naval Division) to come out and join them. This they did, and the two sides exchanged brandy, cigars, whisky, more basic food and mementoes. No officers were present, but later in the afternoon a German major came out, and after discussion with some of our men the two sides were ushered back into their own trenches.

The valley below also saw the exhausted men of the 42nd (East Lancs) Division after they had fought their way through the German defences of the Hindenburg Line at Trescault and battled their way three miles eastwards to this area. On 28 September 1918 they captured Good Old Man Farm with the help of a squadron of 3/Hussars. The commander of the latter, Captain JJ Dobie DSO MC, was killed two days later, on 30 September, and now lies buried in Marcoing Military Cemetery, ID33.

For those who continue this tour on foot, when you proceed past the farm, you will see it is now in ruins - probably not too disimilar to how it appeared in 1917, one feels.

In the early hours of 29 September the New Zealand Division was

42nd East Lancs Division TF with 3rd Hussars
captures farm 28 September 1918

Hussars Captain
Dobie DSO, MC
killed

Good Old Man Farm, having been rebuilt after the war, is derelict again (1995) and probably looking much as it would have done in 1917. The Germans had fortified the buildings and could sweep the slopes with fire.

assembled in Couillet Wood and then came up this slope to attack Welsh Ridge and La Vacquerie, crossing over the chaos of old trenches, wire, unburied dead and gun emplacements.

For those who would prefer to do the next stage **by car,** return to the church and collect your vehicle, and join the tour again at **Villers Plouich Communal Cemetery [6].**

Villers Plouich Cemetery looking up to Welsh Ridge. The cows are grazing at the long communication trench known as 'Surrey Road'. Avenue Trench used to run along the line of the road.

Welsh Ridge

German Line 1917 and 1918

British Line 31 December 1917

Surrey Road

Avenue Trench

For those walking, the track takes you past **Good Old Man Farm [5],** and then close by the points where Wain and Emerson were killed. At the road, turn left towards **Villers Plouich**. It is hard to imagine the thousands of men, horses and vehicles that were assembled in 1917 and 1918 in this valley; or of the lines of stretcher bearers, wounded, maimed and prisoners that came along as the various actions progressed. The south east side of the valley is in dead ground, out of observation from the defenders above.

Just before the railway crossing, and a few hundred yards from the centre of the village, on your left hand side, will be found **Villers Plouich Communal Cemetery**. The cemetery is on the corner of a sunken road, The Avenue; this road connected the D56 (Railway Road) to the long communication trench, Surrey Road, which ran parallel with it, some two hundred and fifty yards behind the cemetery.

At the head of the cemetery may be seen the Cross of Sacrifice, standing as a protective sentinel over a single row of military graves and Special Memorials to men whose graves were lost in later fighting. There are forty five here who fell between November 1917 and January 1918, most killed at La Vacquerie, though there are two from 1916. The thirty seven Germans who were originally buried here have been removed and are now buried at the local German concentration cemetery at Cambrai. There are eight unnamed graves; the forty three identified ones are men from the three divisions of the 1917 battle, and twelve from the RND. The 1916 casualties are Private TG Marshall of 1/East Lancs, captured at Ligny Harcourt and who died as a PoW and Captain Tom Rees, RFC, who was shot down on 17 September 1916.

Walk into the village and take the minor road to Beaucamps. Just past the Mairie, some distance along the narrow sunken road, you will find the eponymous **Sunken Road Cemetery [7]** on your right. The cemetery holds fifty-one men, three of whom are unidentified. The road would have provided the sort of shelter and relative security essential for an Aid Post. Twenty one of the men are from the RND, notable amongst them being Petty Officer HC Williamson (A45) who in his 21 years managed to win the MM and Bar.

Return down the sunken road to the village. It was probably in the cellar of the Mairie that Major-General de Lisle made his HQ after his hasty and narrow escape from Quentin Mill on the morning of 30 November. Take the road to Gouzeaucourt and then the first on the left, the La Vacquerie road. After half a mile or so, just as the road begins its climb up the ridge, you will see the cemetery signpost on the right hand side of the road.

Fifteen Ravine Cemetery.

Fifteen Ravine Cemetery [8] is on the same spot as the 1917 British second line trench, Frimley Trench, running across Farm Ravine, itself used as a communication trench. From it runs a sunken track, again a communication trench, to Gonnelieu. The cemetery got its name from the shallow ravine behind the cemetery, once bordered by fifteen trees.

This is undoubtedly a most beautiful cemetery, and as for so many in this area, relatively rarely visited. It was started in the spring of 1917 by those Welsh regiments who had pushed the Germans back to this area. By the time the Germans overran the cemetery, during the spring offensive of late March 1918, 107 men had been buried here, all to be found in Plot I on the right hand side. After the Armistice, when the battlefields and other small cemeteries had been cleared, 1,005 men were brought here. It also contains two German soldiers at the top right hand side and Special Memorials to the forty-four soldiers who are believed to be buried in this ground. The total of unnamed graves is 740, men who were probably left out on the battlefield for a year, their bones and identification scatterd by time and conflict. This cemetery is the largest in our area of the Right Hook.

There are men from the 12th and 20th Divisions in Plot B. Amongst these is Lieutenant-Colonel Alderman DSO, commanding officer of 6/RWK of 37 Brigade, who fell leading the attack on Le Quennet Farm, just below Lateau Wood. Two of his young officers, Lieutenant WM

Boucher and Lieutenant GT Carre, lie close by.

In IVC15 is the padre of 60 Brigade, Rev OA Holden, killed in the German counter attack of 1 December; next to him is Rev Thomas Howell, the chaplain of 6/KSLI, killed on the same day. There is probably an error in the date of death of Private Fred Riley (IIF18), 28 February 1918. On that day his battalion was at Givenchy, miles away; almost certainly he was killed on 28 September 1918 when the battalion was in action on Welsh Ridge. There are sixteen other men from the 42nd (East Lancs) Division, men killed in the capture of Good Old Man Farm.

In IIIB17 is Sergeant TH Waghorn of 6/RWK, the son of William and Emma Waghorn of Snodland, Kent, killed on 25 November 1917; in VE16 is Private CF Waghorne of XII/Lancers, the son of William and Emma Waghorne of Maidstone, Kent, killed on the same day. Were they brothers? If so, what a terrible day for William and Emma.

Continue your walk up the hill to La Vacquerie, crossing No Man's Land on Cemetery Ridge. The ground which you are walking was crossed by 36 Brigade, heading towards Bonavis Farm. Over to the right, beyond the main road, was 35 Brigade, heading towards the north of Banteux. The small road running south west out of La Vacquerie meets the main road, the D917; close by was the site of a German strong point, The Barricade, also known as the Barracks (on the French map Les Baraques). The place has been rebuilt.

Turn left **[9]** to La Vacquerie (La Vacquerie Road) and rejoin your car.

Tour 2: La Vacquerie to Bonavis

The tour starts at La Vacquerie. It covers the defence of La Vacquerie in December 1917, the right flank of III Corps and the New Zealand Division's attack in September 1918. Allow a morning or an afternoon for this tour, especially if detailed cemetery visits are planned.

Proceed south west out of the village, a short stretch leading to the main road. Parallel to the road lay, three hundred yards to the west, the British Fern Trench and on the left the German Berlin (or Barrier)

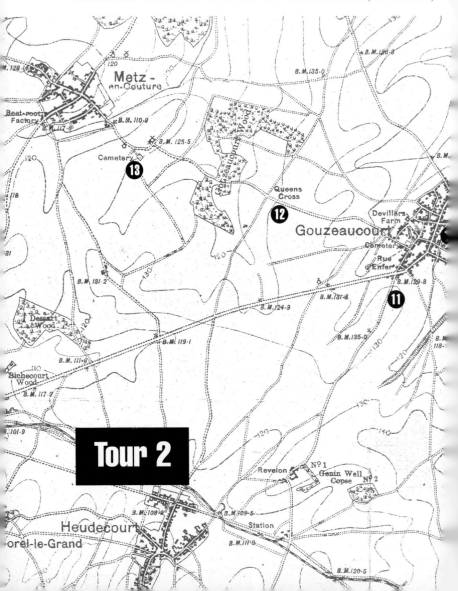

Trench. At the junction, stop **[1]**: a hundred yards or so on the left may be seen the rebuilt building which was the German strongpoint The Barricade. The land to the right is Cemetery Ridge.

Look ahead towards Gonnelieu. On the second night of the British offensive, 21 November, 12 Division turned to face right to form a defensive flank to the south of the main road, the D917. 37 Brigade was brought out of the line into reserve on the land behind you, between the village and Villers Plouich, having the benefit of relatively sheltered ground from the enemy. 36 Brigade advanced a mile to the left, crossing this main road at Bonavis Farm, heading down towards

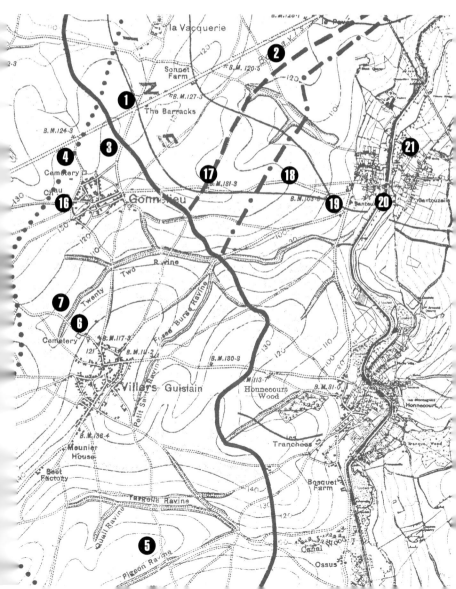

Banteux. 35 Brigade was across the main road before you and dug in where the autoroute cuts across the Hindenburg Line; they stayed there for the next nine days, until the German counter stroke began in this southern sector, three divisions heading from below towards you, preparing to attack the three thousand yard front of the depleted 12th Division. In the land before you 7/Suffolks were effectively destroyed. Gonnelieu, at this stage, had not yet fallen.

Several hundred yards up the main road, [2] where the autoroute goes below it, the HQ staff of 8/R Fusiliers, led by Lieutenant-Colonel NB Elliott-Cooper DSO MC, charged over the road in an attempt to rescue his battalion trapped before Banteux. Successful, the remnants withdrew to La Vacquerie, but perforce leaving him badly wounded and to die in captivity, a posthumous winner of the VC.

Continue towards **Gonnelieu.** In the open ground before the fork in the road, [3] just before the village, were Gun and Gun Support. Here Lieutenant Wallace won his VC and the surviving gunners of Battery C/63 the DCM. His guns blazed away here over open sights, and at the last moment they gathered the breech blocks and sights, quite likely running along this road, and headed for the sanctuary of La Vacquerie.

Brigadier-General CS Owen of 36 Brigade made his escape at that time from Gonnelieu and headed off to Villers Plouich; the village fell to the Germans later that day, 30 November.

Take the right fork and at the T Junction turn right; in a few yards you will come to the village **Communal Cemetery [4]**. There is one of our men here, and one can only hazard a guess as to how often he and his compatriots have been visited. Lance Corporal H Abernathy of 4/Grenadiers, one of Captain Paton's men, killed at the same time as his commander. is buried by the south wall. In the cemetery is the grave of a French pilot killed in 1940; a blade from his propeller is on top of his plot. The Guards Division attacked Gonnelieu from Green Trench, five hundred yards to the west of the village, in a vain attempt to restore it to British hands. Captain Paton won his VC at the west end of the village, near the junction with the Gouzeaucourt road.

Leave Gonnelieu by the D89 to **Villers Guislain** and from there to **Villers Hill Cemetery [5]**.

The cemetery is well signposted in the village, lying half a mile or so to the south east on the crest of a hill and on the right hand side of Gloster Road. It was begun on 3 October 1918 and originally held only a hundred graves, of which some fifty were from 1/Middlesex, mostly killed on 29 September. 35 men are from the Argyll and Sutherland Highlanders, killed in the last few days of that month.

German strong point known as 'The Barracks' looking north to Sonnet Farm, Bleak House and Bonavis.

After the war 628 men were brought in from the surrounding battlefields; they had mostly fallen in 1917 or in the Advance to Victory in 1918. 350 of the graves are unknown; there are 13 Germans, who died as prisoners of war.

There are two members of the Mhow Brigade, 4th Cavalry Division. On 1 December 1917 at 9.35 am the Brigade began its attack, led by the Inniskilling Dragoons, south of Villers Hill. In their charge, hammered by machine-gun fire, the Dragoons lost six officers and 180 other ranks. Private JD Watson is in IIB2; Captain CJB Bridgewater is remembered in a Special Memorial. The rest of their dead are probably represented amongst the unknown buried here.

This, too, is a beautiful cemetery, both in its site and its care.

Return to the village and take the D16 towards Gouzeaucourt, to the north west. A few hundred yards outside of the village stop at the **Communal Cemetery [6]**, on the left hand side of the road. The Cross of Sacrifice is found against the far south wall. To the west may be seen Gauche Wood, off this tour route, but still containing remnants of trenches and bunkers.

There are fifty-one men buried here, seven of whom are unidentified. Amongst the graves there are some of Vincent's men – three of them lie in Plot A. Grave 2 is Corporal WH Britt of 5/Berks, close to one of his officers, Lieutenant TP Wickett. In grave 5 is Private

T Crabb, 9/Essex. They were brought into the cemetery during the battlefield clearance. 18 other men were once buried here with named graves, but these were destroyed by shellfire.

At the corner of a small track, a hundred yards or so along the Gouzeaucourt road on the right, was where Brigadier-General Vincent had his HQ [7]; from here he made his escape across to Gauche Wood, the railway embankment and cutting beyond and finally off towards Gouzeaucourt.

During 30 November the 34th (German) Division took Gonnelieu and then moved on to occupy Gouzeaucourt. However 1/Irish Gds, coming from Metz en Couture, ejected them by late afternoon, the village thereafter remaining in British hands until March 1918.

Proceed for about a mile, passing **Gauche Wood [8]** off to the left. On the left you will see, close to the road, a farm surrounded by trees. Here once stood **Quentin Mill [9]**, whence Major-General de Lisle made his somewhat undignified escape on 30 November, moving his HQ to Villers Plouich.

Cross the railway line; on the outer limits of the village there is a minor road crossing the road; turn right and about a hundred yards on the left hand side you will find a large red brick building, the back wall of the Mairie **[10]**. In its wall, facing east, are the remains of a large British bunker. This now acts as an inconvenient block to the footpath; in 1917 it would have had good fields of fire over to the east and the advancing Germans, though these are, of course, now obstructed by housing.

Return to the original road and proceed into the village, meeting the D917 as it comes through the village. Turn left and at the outskirts of the village left again where you will come to **Gouzeaucourt New British Cemetery [11]** on the left.

This is a large cemetery. At the far end, by the Cross of Sacrifice, are Special Memorials to thirty four British and New Zealand men believed to be buried here. Originally the cemetery only held 55 men, buried to the front and to the right of the gate, in Plot III. After the war a further 1200 or so were gathered in, almost 400 of which are unknown. The most unusual burials are the two Russians, presumably liaison officers with the British. There are many Guardsmen, hardly surprising given the heavy fighting that their Division was involved in both here and at Gonnelieu. The New Zealand casualties were mostly killed during the battle for Trescault Ridge in September 1918.

The oldest man in the cemetery is Private F Garrett of 13/Welsh R (IID6), killed almost at the end of the war, in September 1918, at the

The British Bunker at Gouzeaucourt is a serious obstruction to pedestrians.

age of 47. The fact that he came from Maida Vale shows something of how regiments had moved from the territorial affiliation ideal as the war progressed. Members of Vincent's Force are also here – such as Second Lieutenant WW Freeman, killed in the withdrawal from Gauche Wood, in Plot IV or Private HP Blackie, 6/Queen's, in VIID2. A gallant CSM, A Loveday DCM and Bar, of 1/Wilts, killed on 18 September 1918, is buried in VIIIE17. Second Lieutenant Tack DCM MM, commissioned in the field, was killed on 18 September and now lies in IVA8.

Return to the junction with the D917 and go straight across and then take the first left, the D29b. This is the road used by the Guards when they came to retake Gouzeaucourt and attack Gonnelieu. You are now moving over the September battlefield. The first, deeply sunken, minor crossroads a couple of miles down the road is the old German strong point of **Queen's Cross [12]**. Proceed through the southern part of Gouzeaucourt and a thousand metres or so further on you will come, at a sharp left hand bend, to **Metz en Couture Communal Cemetery Extension [13]**. This is another example of the thoughtful and imaginative care of the British and Commonwealth war dead, the hallmark of the CWGC.

The cemetery lay behind British lines after the German withdrawal of late spring 1917. Many field ambulances were based in the nearby village. After the Germans retook the village in 1918 it was recaptured by the New Zealanders in September 1918. The Germans came close to capturing it in December 1917 – it was an initial objective, in fact, for the first day of their counter offensive. During the battle the Guards Division had their HQ in the village.

There are some five hundred buried in the cemetery; on the east side of the cemetery there were 252 German graves, but these have been removed to Cambrai. Twelve of them remain, however, amongst the British dead. There are several of the defenders of La Vacquerie lying here. Sergeant J Clark DCM of 6/KSLI, killed on 1 December 1917, is buried in IID4; Private W Jordan of 1/RMLI (Royal Marine Light Infantry) is in IIF2 and close by, in F2, is another marine, a member of their Machine Gun Company, Corporal Harry Nutter. He is a distant relative of the co-author, Jack Horsfall. Captain GH Paton VC MC, aged only 22, whose story has already been outlined, lies close to the road in Plot II.

Several senior naval officers, killed in the defence of La Vacquerie, are buried close together. Lieutenant Commander PHS Shaw, Legion of Honour, Croix de Guerre, the 29 year old commander of Hood Battalion, RND, was killed on Welsh Ridge on 30 December 1917 (IIE1). Commander C Skeffington West DSO, commanding the Howe Battalion lies close to his Second in Command, Lieutenant Commander AU Campbell MC and Croix de Guerre.

A quite common sight in the various CWGC cemeteries is the graves of the members of the Chinese Labour Corps, many killed during the clear-up operations after the war ended. Up in the top left hand corner (A3) is Chen Wen, killed on 5 February 1919.

Now return to Gouzeaucourt, turning right at the T Junction and then left on to the D917, driving through the town. On the north eastern outskirts of the village **stop [14]** at the junction with the railway.

A fully laden British supply train was captured on 30 November on your right, at a point where it is clear the station used to be; so were a party of American Railway troops, a number of whom were killed. The German 34th Division had suffered so much in its advance, especially in the loss of officers, that it was unable to continue its advance to Metz. Coming up to the assistance of Vincent's Force came some cavalry (20/Hussars and Royal Scots Greys), whilst 1 Guards Brigade, under the command of Brigadier-General CR Champion de Crespigny, was also being deployed to eject the Germans. De Crespigny rode up to Gouzeaucourt Wood from Metz and decided to attack, even though

Brigadier Vincent's HQ dugout

Withdrawals

GERMAN
34TH DIVISION

Gouzeaucourt and Gauche Wood

Site of Brigadier General B Vincent's HQ, 35 Brigade, 12th Division.

he had no artillery. However, he was able to make his successful attack with the help of a few tanks that did turn up.

If you walk up the disused railway line to your left some three hundred yards, you will find on the right hand side a **quarry[15]**, fenced off and filled with bushes and trees. 6/KSLI were hurriedly brought up to it from their reserve position at Villers Plouich early on

Queens Cross.

1st Guards Brigade at Metz
advanced to retake Gouzeaucourt
30 November 1917

Gouzeaucourt Wood

GERMAN REDOUBT
SEPTEMBER 1918

Guards advance
30 November 1917

Occupied by Germans
30 November 1917

Recaptured by Guards
Division and Ambala Cavalry
Brigade 1 December 1917

Gauche Wood

Brigadier Vincent and 100
stragglers withdraw 30
November 1917

Gauche Wood.

30 November, capturing it from the Germans who were in occupation.
They, 1/Irish Gds and 11/DLI formed a defensive flank running up on
the left to the higher ground west of La Vacquerie. This is a good time
to look at the battle map showing the position of the final Flesquieres
Salient line as it crossed the road near Gonnelieu.

**Quentin Mill in Copse on sky line. 29th Division HQ and scene of Major
General de Lisle escaping capture. He came down the road towards the
camera on his way to Villers Plouich.**

Germans enter
Gouzeaucourt 30
November 1917

Coldstream Guards
recapture Ridge and Mill
1 December 1917

Quentin Ridge

Quentin Mill

Railway Line

Take the right hand turn at the railway crossing, the D96 to Gonnelieu. At the water tower was the old front line of the salient, held until 21 March 1918. The trench crossing the road was Gin Trench; and nearby **Paton** won his VC [16].

Drive through the village, past the church and take the road to Banteux. On 30 November Gonnelieu was a total ruin. The 12th Division was spread out in front of you, and this is the area in which 7/Suffolks was effectively wiped out. A track running diagonally across the road marks the front edge of the Hindenburg Line, where the defence system was five hundred yards deep [17]. The Quarry [18] where 5/Berks and 9/Essex of 35 Brigade tried to hold off the German assault for La Vacquerie was to the left of the road, more or less now engulfed by the autoroute

About three quarters of a mile after the autoroute crossing the **communal cemetery [19]** will be seen on the right; in and around it were no less than eight lines of barbed wire and a plethora of trenches to protect the village. The struggle of 12th Division and the Germans on 30 November was taking place on your left. Amongst those fighting were 7/Norfolks; despite their additional machine-guns they could not stem the German tide. Amongst their dead was Colonel Gielgud, whose body was never recovered.

Drive into the village and **park** as close to the canal as possible, near the bridge. Follow the towpath in a northerly, downstream, direction, to a lock at a point where the canal narrows [20]. This is the one which Sergeant Fitzgerald saved by removing the mines and fuzes. He returned to the main bridge where he surprised the German demolition men, and then proceeded to cross the bridge himself. He then went into Bantouzelle before returning over the bridge and back to his battalion. 2/Canterbury then moved down to secure the canal and the right flank.

Return to your car and drive over the bridge into **Bantouzelle**. at the T Junction turn left (D103) and in less that two hundred yards the **Communal Cemetery [21]** will be seen set back on the right.

There are three British soldiers here, on the south west side, almost hidden by trees, buried together. Have they been forgotten by everyone except the CWGC gardeners?

They were killed on 26/27 August 1914 in the Retreat from Mons; Privates E Magee and Peter McBally, 1/RIR (Royal Irish Rifles) and W. Massey of 2/L Fusiliers.

Follow the road out to the N44; a left turn will take you to the **Bonavis cross roads**.

Tour 3: Bonavis Farm – Ligny en Cambresis.

This car tour will take the visitor to the battles at the St Quentin Canal and the River Escaut (the southernmost part) in November and December 1917 and September and October 1918. There is also a special visit to the scene of a battle involving 1/East Lancs in August 1914; and to the grave of a mother buried close by her son. He was an Australian, quite likely the first killed in the Great War.

A 1914 Action.

This is a section which definitely repays reading before you commence on the tour.

During the last week of August the British and French armies were falling back before the German onslaught as it headed inexorably southwards towards St Quentin and beyond. Cambrai was occupied and the French abandoned Peronne on 27 August. However, the French maintained cavalry patrols in the region, assessing the enemy's strength, dispositions and trying to foresee his intentions. They were back up here again after the battles of the Aisne and the Marne. During that September elements of the 16th Dragoons crossed the canal at the lock bridge at Vaucelles, patrolling eastwards towards Crevecoeur and Harcourt. Whilst engaged in this activity they gained intelligence from M Juste Davenne of Rumilly, assisted by the 19 year old M Maurice Hardouin, who had been invaluable in giving information as to what was happening in Cambrai. From these men the French learned that a German convoy of 26 lorries would be carrying looted goods from Cambrai south, through Masnieres, to Chauny, passing the Bonavis crossroads at some stage in the middle of the morning.

The French prepared a large scale ambush between **Le Quennet Farm [1]** and **Bonavis Farm [2]**, manned by the 16th and 22nd Dragoons, assisted by a group of Chasseurs on bikes. In the courtyard of Bonavis Farm was a French 75 (a formidable, quick firing field gun) and, across the road towards Gouzeaucourt, a reserve of two squadrons of the 16th Dragoons.

As the convoy approached Le Quennet it stopped and two soldiers walked on towards the road junction to see if all was clear. Seeing nothing, they signalled the all clear and the convoy proceeded. When the last vehicle had passed Le Quennet Farm the ambush was sprung and the convoy raked with heavy fire. Whilst the battle proceeded Lieutenant Raoul du Plessis de Grenadin of the 22nd Dragoons approached the first car with a group of his men, in the hope of getting

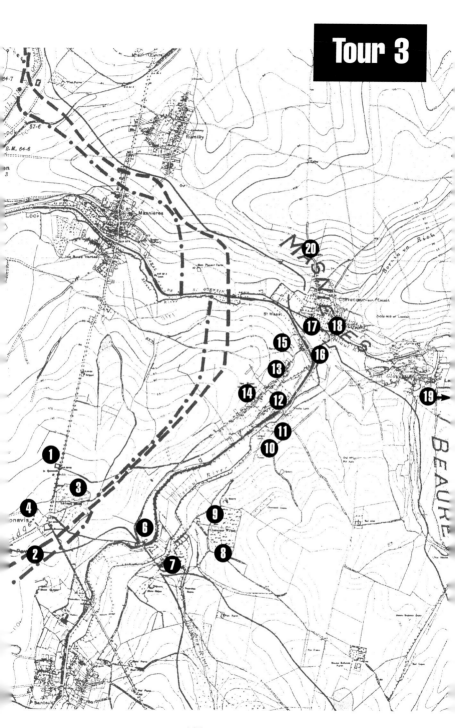

German vehicles carrying looted goods were ambushed by French troops in September 1914. Original small German Cemetery on west side of Road at point of ambush.

the enemy to surrender. Several raised their hands. When he got closer, the officer commanding the convoy stood up and shot the young Frenchman with his heavy calibre revolver, allegedly firing dum dum bullets. Seeing this, the enraged Dragoons proceeded to show no mercy to the enemy. The convoy was destroyed, 34 Germans were killed and 32 wounded. Involved in the ambush were seven British soldiers, who on 10 September had escaped through Crevecoeur and joined up with the French cavalry.

After the French withdrew German cavalry, Uhlans, arrived and

Reprisals for the ambush were carried out on the local populace; buildings in and around Bonavis were torched by Uhlans in 1914. Captured by 6th Buffs 20 November 1917, retaken by Germans 30 November 1917.

proceded to burn down Bonavis Farm and wrecked Le Quennet, not being too gentle with the local popualtion as they took revenge. The Germans buried their dead alongside the road at **Lateau Wood [3]**; this small cemetery was destroyed in the later battles, and if any bodies were discovered after hostilities they would have been removed to Cambrai.

Look west along the D917 towards Gouzeaucourt. A few hundred yards to the right, behind the small circle of trees, is **Pam Pam Farm [4]**. It was captured on 20 November by 6/E Kents with the assistance of ten tanks, whose 6 pdr guns subdued its defences. On 30 November the German counter attack recaptured it, despite 37 Brigade's stubborn defence. Further down the road, on the left hand side, is **Bleak House [5]**, captured by 8/RFusiliers on 20 November after a fierce battle. On the same day Bonavis Farm was shelled by a 15 inch howitzer and Lateau Wood, across the road to the north east, was bombarded by 12 inch howitzers. Bonavis was occupied later that day with little trouble. Beyond Lateau Wood, about eight hundred yards away, on the left hand side of the road, is Le Quennet Farm, captured by 6/RWK. Their commanding officer, Colonel Alderman, killed in the attack, is buried

Pam Pam Farm taken by 6th Buffs 20th November.

Hindenburg Support System taken by 6th Buffs 20 November

Retaken from East Surreys by German 190th Reserve Regiment, 30 November 1917. Lieutenant Baldwin captured

French Ambush September 1914

GERMAN ADVANCE 30 November 1917

at Fifteen Ravine cemetery. The farm was lost on 30 November when 59 Brigade was overwhelmed; Colonel Troughton was captured in his trench, beyond the farm on the left hand side of the road, whilst he was telephoning Brigade. Le Quennet Farm is now a restaurant. There is a track that skirts and goes through Lateau Wood; taking all suitable precautions, especially in the hunting season, it is possible to walk it, and traces of German trenches may be discerned, especially in the late autumn and winter months, when the undergrowth has died down.

Take the turning to **Vaucelles**, the D96. The Germans retained a defence line for the bridge over the canal on this slope, despite the fact that they had been ejected from the high ground by the New Zealanders. Under probing pressure from this Division, and recognising the unsuitability of the position, the Germans withdrew over the canal after midnight, in the early hours of the morning of the 29th September 1918.

Take the right hand fork and park **[6]** at the side of the busy waterway, near the lock and the bridge. The bridge was broken and its western approaches, free of trees and foliage, were swept by machine-gun fire. Lieutenant FK Broadgate was killed here whilst trying to repair the bridge. His body was never recovered, and he is commemorated on the NZ Memorial to the Missing at Grevillers. It was estimated that the Germans had some twenty machine-guns defending the crossing here. It was not until 5/October that 2/Canterbury got a patrol across, scambling over the girders and into

Bridge and lock at Vaucelles.

Lieutenant Douglas 2nd Otago's arrives 4 am 30 September 1918

Captain Hutton 2nd Canterburys first man across 5 October 1918

Lieutenant Broadgate NZ Engineers inspects bridge and is killed

Centre span destroyed

St Quentin Canal flow

Village and bridge →

Abbey at Vaucelles, preserved as the war left it.

the village.

Cross over the bridge and turn left into the village, dominated by a magnificent **abbey [7]**, badly damaged by the war, on the right; it is open to the public. At the end of the village the road turns sharply to the right and up the hill to **Cheneaux Wood [8]**. The fight for the wood, especially up in its **north west corner [9]**, is recounted in the New Zealand chapter of the book.

Return across the bridge and take the right fork for **Les Rues des Vignes**. On 21 November 1917 59 Brigade of the 29th Division came down the slope on the left, having crossed over the N44 to Masnieres; 10/RB led, with 10/KRRC following up.

Go slowly as you enter the village, pass the large factory on the right and keep to the bottom road near the canal and within a couple of hundred yards you will see a narrow path and a small garden leading down to the canal and the **Tordoir Lock [10]**. Walk down to the canal and you will find buildings that similar to, or the same as, the ones that stood here in 1917. Beyond the Tordoir Lock is the **Vinchy Lock [11]**. When the New Zealanders arrived here on 30 September the road bridge and the lock had been destroyed and the low ground alongside the canal was several feet under water. The German defences in the village were such that the Rifle Brigade could make no headway. Two parallel roads run through the village. The church is on the top one, and it was in its vicinity that the KRRC were stopped; in the evening both battalions withdrew from the village and returned up the hill. Close to the church there is the site of a **prehistoric settlement [12]** that may be visited – how it survived the war is almost miraculous. Drive to the top road and then, at the junction with the lower road, you will see a **large farmhouse [13]** which was transformed by the Germans into a fortress.

At this point turn left to visit the **Communal Cemetery [14]**; it is well signposted near the church, and is a couple of hundred yards out on the Masnieres road. There are only two soldiers buried here, both from 2/Auckland, both killed on 30 September. They are Private Robert Hill, aged 21, and an old warrior, even at the age of 25, Second Lieutenant Daniel Slade. He had served in Egypt and Gallipoli and was commissioned from the ranks. In the far corner there is a member of the Chinese Labour Corps, Number 130745, who died on 7 April 1919.

Drive back towards the bridge and turn left just before it. At a point where the road turns sharply to the right, as it drops down towards the canal, **Revelon Chateau [15]** may be seen high up on the left. Stop the car before crossing the **bridge [16]**, parking on the path close to it.

This was the sticking point for the November 1917 operation. The modern, large iron bridge was then of two spans; and there was another crucial one over the Escaut, further to the north east. The failure at the canal bridge put paid to the hopes of the 20th and 29th Divisions, as well as the cavalry; the failure at the bridge over the Escaut was 'the impassable one' for the New Zealanders. Walk over the canal bridge and stay on the road towards **Crevecoeur**. The ground to your right was the marsh; now it is filled with gardens and trees.

At the lock at midday on 21 November a company of 11/KRRC went over a makeshift wooden bridge and faced the enemy across the marsh. Later in the afternoon of the 21st four tanks came down from Revelon Chateau; their machine-gun fire drove the enemy from the canal bridge defences. But as it was dark and the bridge was far from capable of taking heavy weights, the tanks withdrew to the chateau; soon to be followed by 11/KRRC, as the tank support was essential for their further advance. Byng was under the impression that all the suitable bridges in his zone had been destroyed; whatever the reasons, the possibility of crossing here got lost in developments in the battle elsewhere, most notably to the west of Cambrai. Perhaps it could have led to worse trouble if the tanks had chanced things, got across and brought the cavalry with them. The German counter offensive might well have been a major disaster if relatively weak forces had made it

Crevecoeur

German machine guns

L'Escout

Bridge never taken by frontal assault. 59th Brigade failed in November 1917 and 2nd Aucklands failed 30th September 1918

The 'Bridge Too Far' where Private J Crichton won his VC.

across here.

The men of 2/Auckland were out in the open of the 'island', with the remnants of a platoon pinned down by the **stone bridge [17]**. They were utterly exposed to the torrent of German defensive fire. The stone bridge was saved by Private Crichton, and it is easy to see the way his comings and goings would take him as he earned the merit for a Victoria Cross. In the end the bridge was by-passed by the battle, but not before costing 2/Auckland many casualties, not least the Second in Command, Major Edward Sherson, killed whilst trying to find a way for Captain Evans' men to cross.

Drive to the stone bridge, now an iron one. If you park there and look under the bridge it is possible to see traces of the original stone work; and the narrowness of the river. In 1918 it was rather wider and deeper when Crichton slipped into it. The island is gradually being developed, and so this will be a VC action – involving 'the bridge too far' – difficult to understand fully in the years to come; but the heroism of this extraordinary man deserves to live on.

Drive over the bridge and park in

Beneath Private Crichton's bridge the stone work of the original construction can still be seen.

the **village square [18]**. The church is a lovely building and much extended from its pre-war predecessor. This placid place was the scene of the savagery to which war can descend.

From the end of the second week of August refugees from Belgium and north eastern France came through here fleeing from the Germans, bringing with them tales of horror and brutality at the hands of von Kluck's army. On 26 August 1914, strong elements of his 22nd Division advanced on Crevecoeur. Opposing them was a small number of men from the French 5th Cavalry Division. Attacking in the late afternoon, the Germans overwhelmed the French within an hour; leaving 26 of their men dead on the battlefield, the cavalry retreated towards Gouzeaucourt and Peronne. The Germans then set about subduing the local population.

During the morning of 27 August it was alleged that a shot was fired at a Uhlan. It was pointed out that none of the villagers possessed a firearm, but this was of no importance. The village was smaller then, and the roads narrower. Here, in front of the church, the invaders set about throwing bombs into the houses, burning down about forty as a consequence, and rampaging through the street arresting and, in some cases, shooting a number of terrified villagers. Off the village square is a small street, the Rue du Pont de Papier, where Uhlans killed others, using their sabres. In all thirteen were murdered in this fashion; the oldest was 86 and the youngest was a girl of 9, Henriette Lemoine. Their names are on the back of the village war memorial near the church. They then proceeded to round the rest of the population and put them against the long wall of the Convent – the large building to the right of the church on the road to Lesdain.

Preparing to execute them, the soldiers were halted by a mounted officer. The Germans left the subdued village with the dead and wounded lying in the streets and the village on fire. In 1916 the population of the village was evacuated by the Germans, in preparation for it becoming a key element in the Hindenburg Line defences. After liberation by the New Zealand Division the village received the Croix de Guerre. In 1944 it was again liberated, this time by American and French troops.

The next stop has nothing to do with the men of 1917 or of 1918, but is so unusual as to merit the diversion. Proceed on the D15 through Lesdain and Esnes and then visit the **Communal Cemetery [19]** at (Ligny) Haucourt en Cambresis; there is a mass grave of 47 British soldiers from the 1914 fighting here.

Proceed to **Ligny en Cambresis Communal Cemetery** which is

The Church at Crevecoeur and the names of the civilian martyrs of 1914 on the village memorial.

The Pont du Papier – scene of the murders by the Uhlans in August 1914.

Crevecoeur

Massacre of civilians in September 1914

River Escaut flow

clearly visible, with good parking, on the right hand side of the D15 as it passes through the western outskirts of the village, shortly before a crossroad. The Germans also massacred a number of people here in both 1914 and 1940. After passing through the cemetery gate turn immediately left and there you will find a short row of military graves. At the end facing you is that of Lieutenant William Malcolm Chisholm, aged 22, wounded in the battle for the village on 26 August 1914, dying in the village church the next day. The Germans buried him with honour and sent his sword, cap badge and wrist watch home to his mother, via the Red Cross.

His parents were Australians from Sydney who had come to England in 1910 to further the education of their two sons and daughter. William was commissioned into 1/East Lancs after passing through Sandhurst. He was the regiment's first officer to be killed in the Great War. Almost certainly he was the very first Australian to be killed.

His mother and father returned to Sydney in 1919 after their second son, Colin, had recovered from his severe head wound suffered whilst serving with 9/Lancers in the March 1918 withdrawal. Mrs Chisholm was heart-broken at the loss of her eldest son and first born; she was only 63 when she died at her home in Australia in 1928. Her wish was to be buried with her son, and so she was cremated and her husband brought her ashes here. Mrs Emma Isobel Chisholm was the daughter of a French Count; with the blessing of the Mayor it was arranged that her tomb would belong to her family in perpetuity. Her tomb is second on the left of the central path, a big, black, square sepulchre. The flat stone on top is engraved with details of her noble ancestry. This mother and son burial is extremely rare on the Western Front; there are

Ligny-en-Cambresis Communal Cemetery. The ashes of Lieutenant William Malcolm Chisholm's mother are contained in the tomb with the white vase.

other examples, for instance at Estaires in French Flanders. The street leading up to the church is named Rue Chisholm in their memory.

Close to Lieutenant Chisholm there are a number of soldiers of his regiment shown as dying of wounds on 15 January 1915 – Sergeant RJ Carnell, Private George Buckley, Private Robert William Haggett and Private Henry Cowgill. This is unlikely in the extreme – all dying four months after the battle. It can hardly be coincidental that they died one day before the implementation of a warning that all British soldiers evading capture would be treated as spies, together with those civilians hiding them. It is believed locally that after being hidden since August they gave themselves up to save the French family sheltering them; and they were then shot.

Before leaving the cemetery go to the top and there you will find a very ornamental section holding British and French graves beneath large flat stones.

This is a rarely visited cemetery, but is unusual in so many respects that it well deserves the time to remember these brave men and one sorrow-stricken mother.

On your return journey to Crevecoeur stop at the **Communal Cemetery in Esnes**; it is up a minor road. There are buried 112 men of the 4th Division in five mass graves; 62 of the men are unknown. They are all regulars or reservists, members of the famous Contemptible (though to be fair, the Kaiser actually said Contemptibly) Little Army. They would have been buried by the Germans as they cleared the battlefield after the British retreat.

Finally, on returning to **Crevecoeur**, take the turning to the right, the D76 (to Cambrai). A few hundred yards up this road, on the left hand side, is the **Communal Cemetery [20]**; here are buried three men from the RAF, shot down on 16 June 1940.

The graves of the four men of the East Lancashire Regiment believed to have been shot as spies after hiding from the Germans – February 1915 (two in each grave).

Tour 4. Start at Bonavis Farm, then to Les Rues Vertes, Masnieres, Rumilly, the Masnieres-Beuarevoir Line and Crevecoeur

This is a tour which includes five miles walking, depending on whether all the walking options are taken. Parking the car at Les Rues Vertes and walking all of the Masnieres and Rumilly section is advised - and that is where the foot leather will get used! There is a pleasant walk along the tow path towards the end of the tour.

Drive slowly towards Masnieres on the N44, having first looked over the battle maps for the 20th, 21st and 30th November 1917 and those for the New Zealand Division in the autumn of 1918.

On 20 November, on each side of this road, came the 20th (Light) Division to be followed a few hours later by the 29th. Their targets were the bridge crossing the canal and the village of Masnieres and, for the left of the 29th Division, the larger village and the railway station of Marcoing. 59 Brigade crossed this road and headed down towards the canal, whilst the 60th Brigade was spread out on the ridge; by noon 11/RB were at Masnieres Bridge. In due course 88 Brigade led the way of the 29th Division to the canal there, whilst the other two brigades made for Marcoing. On that turbulent morning some 12,000 British troops filled the land around you and to the north; whilst by 11 am the cavalry had been in action, to the left, overrunning a German field artillery position.

At the crossroads a few hundred metres from the village, and just down on the right, is the Ferme des Ecarts. This is close to the site of a German cemetery and now offers Bed and Breakfast accommodation. It has good parking and is an inexpensive and excellent base point for a tour of the Masnieres battlefield.

Head into Masnieres, the part of the village that was known as **Les Rues Vertes** during the war, and find a place to park **[1]** as soon as you can (it becomes built up) and before you get to the traffic lights, which marks the start of the wartime boundary of Masnieres.

Set off towards the bridge. Up the first street on the left, two hundred yards on the right hand side, is the **Brewery [2]**; no longer brewing beer now, it is very similar in appearance to the original structure. This was the area where **Captain Gee** set up his road block on 30 November to deny the Germans access to the **bridge [3]** and village. He then proceeded to clear the village of them and restored British control, aided, at least initially, by only a handful of men. The reinforcements from the far side of the bridge were enough to hold off further German assaults. He was wounded, and later in the day went

144

GERMAN ADVANCE

Gee's advance to cross roads driving Germans back

Captain Gee's barricade

The
Brewery

Cross Roads in Masnieres looking south. The scene of Captain Gee's barricade and battle.

over the bridge, finally making his escape from the relentlessly advancing foe on 1 December when he swam the canal. He well deserved his VC - even the thought of swimming the canal at any time of the year seems bad enough, let alone in the winter.

Down the main street to the bridge came the **Fort Garry Horse**, B Squadron led by Captain Duncan Campbell. They came to a halt when they realised that they would not be able to get over the bridge; but later in the afternoon of the 20th, impatient to get into action, they crossed over the canal by the narrow wooden lock bridge [4], and then charged up the hill.

In 1917 the **main bridge** was made of iron with footways on either side and a wooden foot bridge was alongside. The bridge was damaged when tank F22 made an attempt to cross it, though the result was a great cloud of steam as it fell into the canal and the hot engine and exhaust made contact with the water. The crew was presumably doubtful of the success of the venture, as they took the risk of leaving the doors open; when the water swept over them they were able to make good their escape. They climbed over the broken girders of the bridge and ran for cover to the nearest houses. The last to leave the tank was the commander (perhaps conscious of their alternative name, land ships?), Lieutenant Edmundson. He was a bald headed man who

145

always wore a wig, but lost his hair piece in the escape from the submerged tank. Long after the battle he made a claim for a new wig, saying that the Ordnance issue type was the wrong colour; even more extraordinarily he actually got some money in the fullness of time! According to a crew member of the following tank the Germans did not fire at all as this was taking place. Presumably they were mesmerised by the appearance of the monster, its toppling into the canal, men emerging wearing chain mail and the spectacle of one of them vaguely fishing around for a toupee whilst trying to take cover. Who would not be!?

When the British came into Les Rues Vertes German snipers were still in some of the houses on the approach road to the bridge, and rather more unusually, so were a number of the inhabitants. The German counter offensive preliminary barrage, and subsequent shelling, destroyed most of the village, but some of the houses seem to have survived enough only to require a partial rebuild rather than starting from scratch.

Men of the Rifle Brigade were the first to get here and cross the bridge. When 4/Worcesters arrived they came under very heavy fire (for example from the direction of the church, ahead of you in the distance) and they were soon to lose their commanding officer, Lieutenant-Colonel CS Linton. He is buried at Fins Cemetery, Sorel le Grand; this followed a well-established custom that at the very least officers - and especially the commanding officer - should be got back to the rear for burial. It was a matter of honour and reputation for the battalion concerned. The soldiers on the north side of the canal were held up and could not get forward. Half a mile to the left of the bridge the Newfoundland Regiment found an intact **wooden bridge [5]** and got across. However

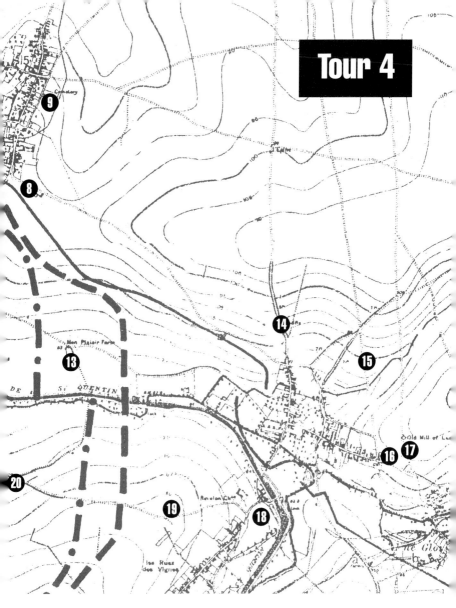

they were held up by an unexpected hazard – a British tank. This had managed to get across at Marcoing and moved on Masnieres, but was disabled by the Germans, A wounded and half blind member of the crew, heroically, carried on firing his machine-gun, but indiscriminately. The soldiers from Britain's oldest colony were the unfortunate recipients of much of this fire.

In another war this bridge was to cause trouble again. On 23

147

The first replacement bridge at Masnieres, damaged in 1944 when an American tank was disabled after crossing.

September 1944 four American light tanks came up to the bridge on the same approach road. They, too, doubted its ability to take the weight of a tank. A young Frenchman, M Bernard Perdix, aged 20, went forward to take a look at it, and was promptly shot for his pains by the German rear guard. A tank then went forward regardless, firing its gun at the church, in front of which was a German anti-tank gun. Just before the tank came off the bridge a mine went off, blowing away one of its tracks. The German rear guard made a hasty departure,

Modern bridge at Masnieres where Lieutenant Edmundson, along with his tank (F22) and crew, fell into the water.

leaving the anti-tank gun behind.

Back to the Great War and the Worcesters; struggling to get on, were reinforced by the 1/Essex, but they could not make much progress during the 20th; the Germans were eventually evicted from the church and its crypt on 21 November.

Walk down the footpath to the canal, where you can get a better impression of the the infantry's difficulties; on the right there is an open flat area on the far side of the canal swept by machine-gun fire. Further along to the right of the bridge, a few hundred yards distance, is the lock bridge over which the Fort Garry Horse managed to cross.

At this point those who wish to continue the tour by car should return to it.

Cross over the bridge and pass the large war memorial, an unusually large and impressive arrangement. At the traffic lights, before the **church [6]**, turn right and then take an almost immediate left to Rumilly. This takes you over the Masnieres-Beaurevoir Line, a very strong German defence system, which was able to defy, for the most part, 29th Division's assaults. To the right of the road **[7]** was where the Fort Garry Horse charged up against the wire of the line, both helped

Entering Masnieres from the direction of Bonavis. The scene of Captain Gee's advance, towards camera, to win the VC.

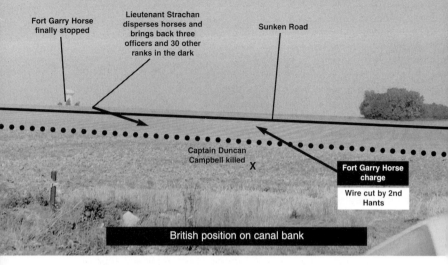

Fort Garry Horse finally stopped

Lieutenant Strachan disperses horses and brings back three officers and 30 other ranks in the dark

Sunken Road

Captain Duncan Campbell killed X

Fort Garry Horse charge

Wire cut by 2nd Hants

British position on canal bank

Looking up the hill to the Masieres-Beaurevoir Line. The water tower and the copse are the scene where the Fort Garry Horse charged and Lieutenant Strachan won the VC.

and hindered by the gathering gloom of the falling night. To the right of the crossroads with the D142, there is a **water tower [8]**. This is where **Lieutenant Strachan** gathered his men and stampeded the horses before getting back through the village and over the canal, his actions during the course of the day winning him the Victoria Cross.

The caribou at Rumilly – the last of such design to be erected in France.

Carry straight on over the crossroads, turn right at the first lane and after four hundred yards or so you will come to **Rumilly Communal Cemetery [9],** on the right.

There are eighty or so men buried here, in eight short rows; only three of them are unidentified. They were all killed in the first few days of October 1918.

Return to the crossroads and turn right, along the D142. This is behind the Masnieres-Beaurevoir Line; in this area 1/L Fusiliers fought to try and stem the German tide on 30 November. They were joined in this endeavour by the Newfoundland Regiment, who had come up this side of Masnieres on 20 November. On the 30th both battalions were forced to fall back to Marcoing, having suffered heavy losses.

If in a car, park as soon as you can after turning left onto the N44 at the T Junction. Walk across to the other side of the road to the **Caribou Memorial [10].** This is one of five set up on the Western Front, the last to be erected in France. The most famous of these stands proudly on a mound, surveying the ground of the Newfoundland Park at Beaumont Hamel. All the Caribou face the direction of the enemy. This one has become somewhat overtaken by what passess for civilization, in the shape of a petrol station.

Walk down the rough track beside the memorial for about a thousand yards, to **Masnieres British Military Cemetery [11]** which is sited on the front of the German defence line. It is an unusual cemetery, for about a quarter of those buried here are German; of the 59 only 19 are identified. These were almost certainly all killed during the fighting of autumn 1918 and cleared after the British had moved on for the final weeks of the war, over to the east. Of the British and New Zealand graves only 16 are unidentified - a clear sign both that the battle had moved on finally from here and that the allies were the victors. The most striking grave, close to the right hand of the entrance, at B21, is that of a young man, already the holder of the MM, **Lance Sergeant Thomas Neely**, killed on 1 October 1918. As a Corporal with 8/King's Own (Royal Lancaster) Regiment he won the Victoria Cross a few days ealier, on 27 September, for extraordinary bravery at Flesquieres.

Walk back to the caribou and then continue the journey into Masnieres. At the traffic lights turn left, onto the D15, towards Crevecoeur, and after several hundred yards, at the **Communal Cemetery**, stop **[12]**. The Sugar Factory was a few hundred yards behind on the south side of the road. Now there are a number of houses surrounding a small square, but, despite the vegetation and trees, it is easy to appreciate the field of fire that was available to the machine-guns of men of the 29th Division that were trained on the open ground on the far side of the canal as the Germans came up to assault Les Rues Vertes from the Rue des Vignes, However, on 1 December the remnants of the defenders of Masnieres were driven westwards, and the village was lost until September 1918.

At this point, if you are walking, it would be sensible to return to your car and take a jump to the next point in the comfort of four wheels.

Note as you drive past the sugar factory area, looking to the left, how the slope commands the canal below; the Masnieres-Beaurevoir Line further up from the road was excellently sited to cover this obstacle.

Drive on for several hundred yards. You will see on the right a small stand of trees just as the road kinks to the left. Stop at this the site of **Mon Plaisir Farm [13]**. Here was the front edge of the German line on 20 November; and the Farm was thought to be a German fortress. On the night of 20 November 11/RB of 59 Brigade crossed the canal by way of the nearby wooden bridge and were surprised to find it empty; they were replaced by 4/Worcesters the following day, the

Mon Plaisir Farm.

Masnieres-Beaurevoir Line

St Quentir Canal Bridg

Mon Plaisir Farm

11/RB occupied empty farm at night

29th Division with posts at road 30 November

Attack up hill from Marcoing at 2.30 pm 20 November 1917.
Stopped at German Main Line

Barbed wire cut by
1st Inniskillings

GERMAN AMMUNITION
PITS IN FIELD
stubbornly defended

Masnieres-Beaurevoir Line

**Hill up which the Inniskillings attacked and Lieutenant Colonel Sherwood
Kelly won the VC.**

riflemen returning to the other side of the canal. This all sounds
straight forward on paper; but it needs to be borne in mind how
terrifying the prospect would have been to the soldiers involved. They
were crossing a waterway at night against the prospect of a hostile
bank, investigating what seemed to be a major stronghold. If they were
outgunned they had every prospect of being sandwiched between a foe
and the canal. If things had gone wrong, the armchair critic would have
called it a hare-brained scheme, reckless and careless of human life.
Because it worked, it becomes a daring exploit, Such is the thin line
between heroic endeavour and skillful action and a disregard for
military reality.

At midday on the 21st lines of German infantry were seen coming
towards the farm from the direction of Crevecoeur, to be halted by the
machine-guns and artillery of the 29th Division. The action took place
on both sides of the road before you.

Mon Plaisir Farm was held until 30 November by 11/Middlesex
when, depleted in number, the remainder exhausted, they were forced
to withdraw towards Masnieres. The wooden bridge no longer exists.
The farm took no further part in the battle; its next allied occupants
was the New Zealand Division.

1/Auckland formed up on the road above the farm (the D142) at 6
am on 1 October 1918, facing eastwards to attack across the open,
sloping valley side, with 2/Wellington below them. The objective for
1/Auckland was a position called the **Crucifix [14]**, which is the

location of the Communal Cemetery of Crevecoeur, on the D76, a sunken road to Cambrai. Initially successful, the Aucklands continued on to a track on higher ground, the **Old Mill Road [15]**, but were forced back by German counter attacks to the D79, to which position the New Zealanders held on. After midday they were relieved by 1/Wellington, whilst 2/Wellington had managed to capture most of Crevecoeur and the north crossing of 'that' stone bridge by 8 am.

Drive in to Crevecoeur and follow the D15 around the church and off to the left in front of it (towards Lesdain). Towards the end of the village's east end, at the last turning to the left, stop by the **crucifix [16]**. It was here that the New Zealand advance was brought to a halt by a hail of bullets and an artillery barrage; no further progress could be made. It was not until the Germans began their withdrawal to the River Selle on 5 October that the whole of Crevecoeur fell and the New Zealand Division could continue its advance.

It is worth your while to make your way up the track leading up to the site of the **old windmill [17]** so that the difficult uphill and open approach of 1/Auckland may be more fully appreciated.

Return to Crevecoeur and cross the bridges over the Escaut and the canal; you might like to park your car immediately after crossing the latter and then walk up the tow path for the half a mile or so to the **St Waast Lock [18]** and the new bridge over the canal; it is a pleasant and peaceful stroll. It was here that 11/KRRC crossed at midday on 21 November and attempted to enter Crevecoeur. They were driven back

Masnieres Lock Bridge over which went the Fort Garry Horse in failing light 3.30 pm, 30 November 1917.

2nd Hants over lock cut gaps in German wire for cavalry

Fort Gar (B Sqd) over loc inte Masr Beaure

Remains of a German bunker near the lock.

and withdrew over the canal to a position on the hill top dominated by Revelon Chateau; the New Zealanders also came over at this point in their advance.

Return to the car and up the steep hill past Revelon Chateau, now obscured with trees, and head for Masnieres and Marcoing. It was down this road that the tanks came to push off hostile machine-guns but then determined that the bridge would not take their weight and they returned back to the chateau area.

At the fork in the road, **stop [19]** and walk up on to the right bank. Looking west you are viewing the ground along which the Germans went on 30 November, only to face the resolute Captain Gee and the machine-guns from the sugar factory.

About a mile further on is the **track [20]** that led down to the wooden bridge to Mon Plaisir Farm. to the north east you should get a glimpse of the lock over which the Fort Garry Horse went. A thousand yards or so further on, on the left, is a **monument [21]**. It was erected by public subscription by the people of Masnieres in gratitude for Lieutenant Theodore Hostetter. He was an American serving with the Royal Air Force who was shot down on 28 September 1918 and buried on this spot by the Germans. After the war his parents reclaimed his remains and took them to the American Somme cemetery at Bony. They gave a large sum of money for the rebuilding of the infants school and for the erection of the town war memorial.

Continuing, just before the cross roads is the Ferme des Ecarts; and beyond that the N44.

Tour 5: Marcoing to Cambrai and Bapaume

This tour takes the visitor through the villages of Marcoing and Noyelles, the northernmost part of the battlefield covered in detail in this book; from there the route is to the German cemetery at Cambrai and via a few, more western cemeteries where 'our' soldiers are buried or commemorated, before directing on to Bapaume and home, or to the Somme, or Artois or Flanders.

Start at the **Ferme des Ecarts** crossroads on the N44. Drive along the narrow sunken road towards Marcoing. On the morning of 20 November 88 Brigade worked its way down the slope on your left and over this road, into Masnieres. At the next **crossroads [1]** carry on towards Marcoing. In the left hand corner of this road was a British battlefield cemetery, which has since been cleared.

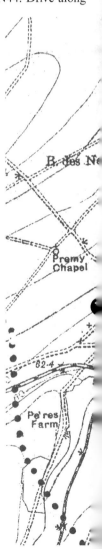

In the drizzling rain the remainder of the Division, 86 and 87 Brigades, worked their way from the area of La Vacquerie towards Marcoing. Nine battalions, including the Pioneers, 2/Monmouths, pressed forward. Four battalions went through **Marcoing Copse [2]**, to the right when the road bends to the right, not far from the canal; the rest passed the western side of Marcoing, heading for Nine Wood and the village of Noyelles, a mile and a half to the north.

You might like to find a convenient spot to stop just beyond the copse, or else drive slowly. At about 10.30 am eight tanks arrived, commanded by Major JC Tilly; he entered the village on foot and was greeted by excited inhabitants. Then he saw Captain Bayley of the same Tank Battalion running towards the **iron railway bridge [3]** over the canal, firing his revolver at a party of Germans who were preparing to blow it up. Dispersing them, he cut the electric leads to the explosives and saved the bridge from demolition. The tanks did not cross because the village was still full of the enemy, who were being dealt with by 87 Brigade, in the area close to the bridge. An advance party of 9/Suffolks (71 Brigade) of the 6th Division, coming from the west, had managed to arrive somewhat earlier and had set about clearing snipers from the house. Meanwhile more tanks had arrived and climbed the railway embankment at the other (north western) side of the copse, and poured fire from their 6 pdrs into the enemy positions in the buildings.

Although no tanks had yet gone over the bridge, still more arrived and 17 of them swung left towards **Nine Wood [4]** and Noyelles. In the area to the left of Marcoing Copse, by this stage in the morning of the 20th, the cavalry had begun to arrive, occupying the fields to the west

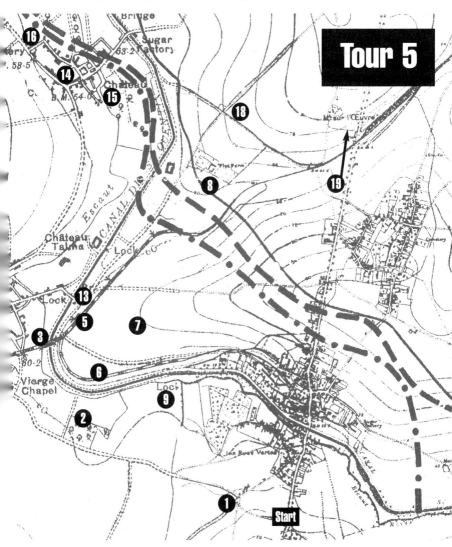

Embankment at Marcoing from which the tanks of Major Tilley fired on the village.

Captain Bayley's bridge which was saved from demolition by the Germans.

and south of the wood, waiting for Marcoing to be cleared before they could progress. In the trees of the copse a number of German snipers were taking a deadly toll; 2/SWB with three tanks were used to clear them.

At the T Junction turn right and go under the railway, and you will see the embankment where the tanks were positioned which shelled the houses. Further to your right, but not yet visible, is the railway bridge over the canal saved by Captain Bayley; at midday on 20 November 1/Border sent A and C Companies across it; once on the other side they made progress towards the railway station.

Continue straight ahead for the centre of the town and then turn right towards the canal and the road bridge. Here is the lock across which Second Lieutenant WG Denareaz of C Company 1/Border went. Once across the canal turn right and immediately take the narrow road on the left and up the bank to the **railway station [5]** (now closed). There is a small square with a very nice little restaurant which also has a number of small rooms for Bed and Breakfast.

Marcoing Railway Station where Sergeant Spackman won his VC.

1st Border
Regiment HQ
night 29
November
1917

Station Restaurant and Hotel.

The large railway complex and buildings were heavily bombed during the Second World War, but there is still the site of the German machine-gun post on the station platform. This was charged by **Sergeant Spackman** of the Borders, capturing the post, killing the three members of the crew and taking the gun intact. His was 1/Border's second Victoria Cross of the war. Walk across to the other side of the station and you can see the platform and the railway line along which he came.

Another hero of the Border Regiment that day was the redoubtable Second Lieutenant Denareaz who, with his platoon, had crossed the lock and captured two more machine-guns; C Company continued to surround the station and eventually established the Battalion's HQ there.

Go down the slip road to the D15 below , and turn left. On the right is the railway bridge which was saved by Captain Bayley and from which Sergeant Spackman attacked. In a few hundred yards you will see the Cross of Sacrifice of **Marcoing British Cemetery [6]** on the right hand side of the road.

This cemetery was created after the war when men were gathered in from the surrounding battlefields and also from the German cemetery that then existed in Rumilly. There are just under 350 men buried here, of whom just under a third are unknown. Most of these would have been killed in the 1917 battles and lain out all through the winter; a number of these were from the 63 (Royal Naval Division), killed in the desperate fighting around Welsh Ridge right at the end of 1917. At the end of the rectangular plot, behind the Cross of Sacrifice, are memorials to twenty four men who are believed to be buried here.

Although intrinsically sad, this is an interesting cemetery, with representatives of men from all over the world. 52 are from the 29th Division, which fought so hard to take the canal and river crossings and then held them against the German onslaught of early December 1917. Eight men are from the Canadian Cavalry, the Fort Garry Horse, who charged the barbed wire at Rumilly. Their commander, Captain Cameron, is buried at Flesquieres. These men were quite likely buried in Rumilly German cemetery originally; and there are men from Newfoundland as well, at that stage, of course, not part of the Canadian federation. Over forty men are from New Zealand, many of whom would have died in the attempt to take the bridge at Crevecoeur. The oldest man in the cemetery is **Major Edward Sherson** of 2/Auckland, aged 51 (IE23); he was killed on the marshy island before Crevecoeur, trying to find a way out for his men.

Scene of Sergeant Spackman's charge.

Captain JJ Dobie DSO MC, 3/Hussars, aged 41 (IB33) was killed on 30 September 1918 after assisting 1/8 L Fusiliers (42nd (East Lancs) Division) capture Good Old Man Farm on the slopes of Welsh Ridge. **Second Lieutenant FHA Weale** (IIE20/21) was a 19 year old pilot from 57 Squadron in the RAF who was shot down on 2 October 1918; he had come all the way from Sao Paolo, in Brazil, to enlist.

Before leaving the cemetery, look north eastwards up the slope towards the Masnieres-Beaurevoir Line and towards Masnieres Military Cemetery; this is the ground **[7]** over which **Lieutenant-Colonel Sherwood-Kelly** led his Inniskillings in the afternoon of the first day, cutting barbed wire by hand and capturing fifty prisoners and five machine-guns and winning the Victoria Cross for himself.

On the second day of the battle eighteen tanks crossed the canal at its sharp bend, to your rear, and pushed forward uphill to the Masnieres-Beaurevoir Line, machine-gunning the enemy trenches; they did not break through and were badly mauled by German field guns and armour-piercing bullets, losing seven of the tanks in their attempt.

Later in the day 5/Dragoon Guards arrived and a squadron went forward to try and get in touch with a company of 1/Border which had gone up the hill behind a tank towards **Flot Farm [8]**, a building that

B Company 1st Border crossed here led by Second Lieutenant Dendreaz.

The view Second Lieutenant Dendreaz would have had of the railway station high on the bank.

stands about a mile in front of you, to the north.

On 3 December, at the height of the German counter-offensive, on both sides of the canal, 88 Brigade and 2/SWB in particular, lent to them by 87 Brigade, suffered very heavily.

Walk a hundred yards or so up the road from the cemetery, towards Masnieres, and take the small, curving path on the right going down to the **Lock** (French *Ecluse*) **de Bracheux [9]**. There was a shallow trench near to the Lock House, the scene of most bitter fighting on 3 December. The Germans held the Lock House when it was attacked no less than three times by 14/DLI led by **Captain AM Lascelles,** although he was wounded three times in the process. Captured by the Germans he managed to escape, quite remarkably, and then rallied his men again. The men were forced to withdraw down the hill and over the canal; the indomitable Captain winning the Victoria Cross for his heroic actions. As so often on the battlefields today, it is hard to imagine such desperate fighting taking place in a spot where huge barges and pleasure cruisers slide sedately pass on the calm waters.

Lock de Bracheux, scene of Captain Lascelles' attack and his VC.

Marcoing Communal Cemetery.

Turn around and go back over the canal bridge below the railway station and head towards the church; just behind it, two short streets away up the hill on the narrow road that rings Marcoing is **Marcoing Communal Cemetery [10]**, on the northwestern corner of the village. The cemetery was used by the Germans in 1917 when they retired behind the Hindenburg Line; their 129 men were removed in 1919. Eight British PoWs who were buried here by the Germans were also removed and reinterred at St Souplet, not far from Le Cateau.

In a small square plot amongst the civilian graves are 13 unkown British soldiers and 11 Special Memorials to 'lost graves', all killed during the Cambrai battle. Four men are known, one of whom is Second Lieutenant Yates, aged 19, of the Hampshires; he was killed on 22 November.

When you leave the cemetery continue up the road, stopping by the **crucifix [11]** right at the north west corner of the village, just as the road makes a sharp bend to the right. To the north, a few hundred yards ahead and on a slight rise, is Nine Wood. 17 tanks of H Battalion went over these fields on 20 November, crossing the D15, a couple of hundrded yards in front of you. They were followed by 16/Middlesex and 1/R Guernsey LI, the latter taking part in its first action of the war. In the top left hand corner of the wood, where there is a square of open land behind a **quarry [12]**, are signs of German trenches. From these they knocked out some of the tanks before the British finally occupied the wood. A squadron of 7/Dragoons also came into the wood.

Proceed slowly on the D29 towards Noyelles; when you have passed the houses and the wood is not too far off to the left, where the road bends, there is a track off to the left whilst another one to the right leads down to the **Lock de Talma [13]**, just below and to the north of the railway station.

The road into **Noyelles** (occupied on the first day) is in the footsteps of the Royal Fusiliers, with the Middlesex on their left. Take the first road on the right and park by the **church [14]**. The river runs through the **chateau grounds [15]** (itself a ruin) on the right. The bridge was demolished by the Germans and the Fusiliers found it

'Impossible' Bridge 800 yards

Noyelles Church.

impossible to reach the iron bridge over the canal some five hundred yards further on. The Germans actually occupied the bridge whilst all its approaches were swept by machine-gun fire from the factory buildings on the far side.

The old red brick wall surrounding the chateau is original and shows the scars of shell and machine-gun fire. The Royal Fusiliers went into the grounds, established posts and then found a wooden bridge over the river was still intact; they were joined by a squadron of 4/Dragoons.

Return to the D29 and turn right; about five hundred yards further on, on the right hand side and at the edge of the village, is **Noyelles sur l'Escaut Communal Cemetery and Extension [16]**. There is only one man in the Communal section, in the bottom left hand corner; it is a frequent question as to why the odd individual or couple of individuals are left in the communal part of a cemetery when there is a military extension adjacent. He is Lieutenant WB Cramb of the RFC, who was shot down near here and buried by the Germans on 14 April 1917.

The Military Extension is behind the hedge, clearly indicated by the Cross of Sacrifice. There are 115 burials, only four of whom are unknown; they are men, for the most part, from the 2nd, the 62nd (West Riding) and the 63rd (Royal Naval) Divisions who fell in the Advance

German bunkers.

The untakeable bridge.

Noyelles 500 yards

German-held bridge

Sugar factory
with original shell
damaged wall

to Victory in September and October 1918. Private M Tester (Row A9) was one of 36 men of 17/R Fusiliers killed in the canal crossing here on 28/29 September 1918. He was from East Grinstead and must only have been a schoolboy (or rather, of modern schoolboy age) when he enlisted, for he was only 17 when he was killed. Nearby is Private ME Tickner, 24 R/Fusiliers, aged 36, whose wife lived in Paddock Wood. However his parents lived in Carlisle, Concord Lowell, in the USA. There would seem to be an interesting personal story here.

On the opposite side of the road there are a row of deep concrete bunkers in the bank; these were used as barracks and ammunition storage - a large number of Germans were caught unaware in these positions, many still asleep, by the British in 1918. Walk up the **narrow road** nearby **[17]** and the strength of the Masnieres-Beaurevoir Line at this point is clear to see.

The Germans, loathe to leave Noyelles in British hands, mounted a counter attack at 10.30 am on 21 November 1917. They came from the eastern side and got as far as the church and the into the chateau grounds. With the help of a squadron of dismounted 9/Lancers, 1/L Fusiliers and 2/R Fusiliers with the assistance of two tanks, regained the village by nightfall. The village was lost on 5 December in the final withdrawal into the Flesquieres Salient.

Turn around and return past the church and drive over the St Quentin canal, immediately afterwards turning right down the D142. After about a mile stop at the **crossroads [18]** and look to the right; some three hundred yards away is Flot Farm, hidden by trees. The drive along this road has taken you through the Masnieres-Beaurevoir Line, with two lines of trenches a hundred yards apart crossing the road before reaching the crossroads.

Follow the D142 to Rumilly and on its north western edge turn left on the N44 to Cambrai **[19]**. When the road runs out, on entering Cambrai, take the right turn for Valenciennes and Solesmes. Keep going, looking for the sign to Solesmes, the D942, the Route de Solesmes. En route you will have crossed railway lines and run alongside large expansive marshalling yards. Almost as soon as you are on this narrower road, and just beyond the road sign, on the right behind a stone wall, is **Cambrai German Military Cemetery** and **Cambrai East Military Cemetery.** There are several cemeteries on the Western Front of similar composition – British, German, French and occasionally Russian burials - for example at Mons and Le Cateau; but this one is overwhelmingly dominated by the thousands of Germans buried here. The contrast of the cemetery styles is quite stark.

French helmet

French graves with 250 Russian soldiers of 1916

German graves

German Cemetery Cambrai.

Of course, not only did Germany lose one war, she lost two. Her dead were most respectfully buried during the course of the war by their compatriots - clear evidence of this may be seen in the remnants of German headstones at Sanctuary Wood Museum, near Ypres. The end of the Second World War was the point at which 'host' nations determined that enough was enough, and many smaller German cemeteries were concentrated. Thus, the small German cemetery at Polygon Wood, beyond the British one there, was one of a number that was concentrated to Langemark, bodies bulldozed into a quite extraordinarily small space. Until some fifteen years or so ago there was no visible sign in the cemetery as to who was buried in this obscene pit that holds over 20,000 burials, About that time the Germans made earnest efforts to improve this sad situation - new crosses in some cemeteries, of iron, rather than wood; lists of name cast in metal listing the known dead in mass graves. But the fact remains that German cemeteries are stark, magnificent and desolate in their vastness and regularity. This, too, is something shared to a large extent by the French. A secular state dominated by Christianity, its soldiers were given single burials but also in uniformity; a state that has seen fit, so I have been told, to destroy cemeteries in the recent past for purposes of convenience. Thus far the British have stood alone in retaining an enormously expensive sysytem of leaving everyone where they were, so far as practicality allowed, and treating each grave in an individual way. The Americans had the option of having their loved ones repatriated to the United States; their cemeteries on the Western Front can also be anonymous, stark and regimented, but are usually accompanied by great expenditure on beautiful lawns, reception areas, explanatory maps and chapels. A recent Minister of Veteran Affairs in France – a good and devout man, who impressed one enormously – argued that his funding should be spent on the living veterans; to which the reply, to my mind, is that these men were asked by their country to be prepared to sacrifice themselves and at the expense of their family, and it does the state no credit if they are now seen to be shallowly treated. I recommend a visit to French cemeteries on the Marne to see how desperate the situation has become. Yet, on the other hand, the French authorities have always been diligent and helpful in every way to the maintenance and well being of British cemeteries - an excellent example of which is the access roads especially constructed for Arras Road and Nine Elms cemeteries near Arras, or the Pont du Jour memorial. A diatribe, maybe, but a point for reflection, and indicative, at least in some way, of national characteristics and experience of conflict.

The Bavarian commander of the town, when he realised that he would lose Cambrai, recorded that he handed the cemetery over to the French authorities for its safe keeping and maintenace. However in the battle, when the town's centre burned for two days, much was damaged. In the cemetery there are some 500 British graves, including

Havrincourt Chateau.

one from the British West Indies Regiment.

Two of them are from 1914, both of them commemorated by a Special Memorial. Rifleman F Macey of 1/RB died on 22 October and Private James Revell of 1/East Lancs on the 24th, both PoWs from the 4th Division battles a few miles to the east, in August 1914. Of the battles covered in the book there appears to be only one (at least on the British side). Private F Lincoln of 7/Norfolks died on 23 July 1918, in VIIA9; he must have been captured at Banteux Ridge on 30 November when his commanding officer, Colonel Gielgud, was killed. In IIIA77 lies the only American, Private T McGill, aged 20, from Delaware. He served with 6/Connaught Rangers and died after the war, in December 1918.

Return towards Cambrai and follow the signs for Arras and Bapaume, the D939 and then the signs for the N30 going across the town. Pass the signs for Proville, on the south western edge of Cambrai and then quite quickly there is a left fork to Bapaume.

Pass through Fontaine Notre Dame, so resonant in the history of the Guards Division, and go south under the great bulk of Bourlon Wood; just beyond the British cemetery to the north of Anneux take a sharp left for Flesquieres. Before Flesquieres you will pass an oblong wood, after which the cemetery on the right hand side beyond it is named, **Orival Wood British Cemetery**, a cemetery which was considerably expanded from the 90 or so in it when *Silent Cities* (published originally in 1929) was produced. Continue another mile or so, and at the T Junction can be seen on a high bank facing you **Flesquieres Hill British Cemetery**. There are just under a thousand British burials here; the 583 German graves that were once here were removed in 1924.

In VIB16 is **Captain Duncan Campbell**, the squadron commander of the Fort Garry Horse who was killed in the charge on the edge of Rumilly on 20 November 1917. 52 of the New Zealanders who fell before Crevecoeur are also here, the largest number from any division in the cemetery. Perhaps a special note might be made of Private Louise Emile Bray, R Guernsey LI, aged 18 in VIIF16; he would have been brought here after the war during the extensive clearance and search for bodies that took place in the immediate post-war years.

Drive into the village and, as you enter, you will find at the village green on the right of the road a large grey memorial stone next to a French monument. The stone was erected by the villagers to record its liberation in 1944 and the action of one man in particular, Corporal Johannes Bergman. He was in command of a troop of the US 113

Memorial to the Missing of the Battles of Cambrai at Louverval.

Reconnaissance Squadron and was the first allied soldier to enter the village, on 2 September 1944. Many photographs were taken of him with his jeep, surrounded by the people of the village on that happy day. Later on that same day his small column drove away on the road to Cantaing; sadly, he was sniped within minutes by a German marksman, being hit when he had reached on the edge of the village. The Corporal, aged 27, was taken to the church and was in due course buried with due ceremony, the whole village following the coffin to the cemetery. In 1948 he was taken home and reinterred at Oak Hill in Parkers Burg, Iowa. He is remembered every year on 2 September on the anniversary of the liberation.

A future addition to the memorials in Flesquieres is likely to be a British tank unearthed by local people under the guidance of a local historian, in November 1998. It seems likely that the tank was shoved into a huge shell crater and used as some sort of shelter or fortification by the Germans. There is reputed to be another tank somewhere within (and under!) the parish boundaries.

From Flesquieres take the road to Havrincourt and then the D15 to reconnect with the N30. This road takes you alongside the Canal du Nord, then uncompleted and empty. Amongst other points of interest are the dugout in which Brigadier-General 'Boy' Bradford VC DSO MC was killed; Sanders Keep cemetery on the right, a small cemetery on ground which was defended by barbed wire metres deep on the slope down towards the canal, in which Lance Corporal Jackson VC is buried. His is one of two VCs won at the same time; several hundred yards further on, near the junction with the D15E in the crossing of the bridge over the canal to the left. The other winner of the VC was Captain Cyril Frisby of the same regiment, the Coldstream Guards.

At the N30 turn left and after a couple of miles, on the right hand side of the road, you will find the Memorial to the Missing in the Cambrai battles at Louverval, though in reality it is isolated by the road side. There is a small cemetery down below the impressive memorial, with its bas reliefs and lists of names, 7,000 of them, well over 40% of those who were killed in the battle between 20 November and 8 December 1917.

It is fitting to spend the last moments of your stay on the Cambrai battlefield at a place quite so poignant at this.

Continue on to Bapaume and home to the UK – or to future battlefield exploration.

British MkIV tank knocked out at Flesquieres and discovered 81 years later in November 1998. It is thought to be D41 and commanded by Second Lieutenant R A Jones. Jones is buried in Flesquieres Hill Cemetery.

INDEX